THE FIVE COMMANDMENTS OF JESUS

THE FIVE
COMMANDMENTS OF JESUS

A NEW APPROACH TO CHRISTIANITY

Patrick J. Amer

www.thefivecommandmentsofjesus.com

iUniverse, Inc.
New York   Bloomington

The Five Commandments of Jesus
A New Approach to Christianity

iUniverse books may be ordered through booksellers or by contacting:

iUniverse
1663 Liberty Drive
Bloomington, IN 47403
www.iuniverse.com
1-800-Authors (1-800-288-4677)

ISBN: 978-1-4401-6224-4 (pbk)
ISBN: 978-1-4401-6223-7 (ebook)

To find out more about the book, to communicate with the author, or to read and
download a Discussion and Study Guide, go to
www.thefivecommandmentsofJesus.com

Printed in the United States of America

iUniverse rev. date: 10/22/09

TABLE OF CONTENTS

TABLES

On the cover: *Jesus Teaching on the Sea Shore,* by J. J. Tissot

INTRODUCTION

How did I come to write this book? Let me give you some background about myself, and then tell you how the book came about.

I was brought up in a devout Catholic family. I received about as much Catholic education as one can get, and I read a good deal of philosophy and theology on my own. After my freshman year in college at Holy Cross, I entered the Jesuit order in 1956 at Milford, Ohio. I left after ten months, partly because I realized that I couldn't live a life of poverty, chastity, and obedience, and partly because the philosophy and spirituality of the order at that time was deeply rooted in the sixteenth century and seemed to me to have no connection with the modern world. I then returned to college, graduated from St. Louis University, and went on to law school at New York University. After law school I returned to Cleveland, where I was a practicing tax and corporate lawyer for forty-one years. I retired in 2004 and moved to Hilton Head, South Carolina.

In the late 1960s and early 1970s, my wife Betty and I drifted away from religious practice, and then from religious conviction, as did so many of our contemporaries. As we saw it, the Catholic Church had missed the civil rights movement, had ignored the anti-Vietnam War movement, and had begun its repudiation of the reforms of the Second Vatican Council (1962-65) which continues to this day. On a more fundamental level, we felt a profound disconnect between the teachings and practices of the Christian churches and the culture of the real world, the modern world. The Christian churches seemed to us to be addressing the modern world in language and with concepts from a different century. Many of these teachings weren't harmful; they just weren't relevant, and they weren't inspiring.

I remember one Sunday afternoon in or about 1970 when Betty and I, who had both taken up yoga, went first to a *puja*, or prayer service, at the yoga ashram in Cleveland Heights, and went from there to a student Mass at John Carroll University, a Jesuit college. The congregation at the *puja* was alive and vibrant. The members participated in the prayers and singing with enthusiasm, fervor, and devotion. In stark contrast, the congregation at Mass was impassive, nonparticipating, and obviously bored. The Catholic Church didn't speak to them, and they didn't respond. In the early 1970s, Betty and I participated for several years in a home Mass group (what would now be called an "intentional Eucharistic community"), which was spirited and inspiring, but when several key couples got divorced or moved out of town, that group broke up, and we stopped going to church at all.

But as with many former Christians, there always remained with me the nagging and troubling question whether I was missing out on something very important. So as I approached retirement I began reading and studying about Christianity again, to see if I could find a spiritual home. I was quite unsure whether I would be able to find a Christianity I could accept, because I started my search with two convictions about the Christian faith which I still hold:

First, I don't accept the traditional Christian teaching that Jesus's death was a sacrifice to atone for Adam's and Eve's sin, and for humanity's sins. I can't accept a God who demanded, desired, or required the torture and death of Jesus, and I think it's apparent from all Jesus said that he wouldn't have accepted such a God either. I can't imagine a God who would say to humanity, "You know I was very upset and angry when Adam and Eve ate the apple, and I punished you all for that. But when you tortured and killed my only Son, it pleased me, and it made everything right again." As I don't believe that one person can assume the moral responsibility and moral guilt of another person, so I can't believe that Jesus took our sins upon himself or that he died for our sins.

Second, I can't accept the Adam and Eve story. God didn't create humanity in a state of original perfection, which God then took away when Adam and Eve ate the forbidden fruit. All of biology, anthropology, and paleontology show that the human condition has always been much as it is now, as we struggle with evil, face natural and man-made disasters, and end this life in death.

So I found myself searching for an acceptable understanding of Christianity which didn't include these traditional teachings. I wasn't at all confident I could find such an understanding, or that one was there at all. Among other problems, I saw that if I rejected the teaching that Jesus came to die for our sins, substituting himself for the rest of humanity in making atonement to God, I raised several difficult questions: What then did Jesus come to do? How does what he actually did redeem humanity? What did he redeem humanity from?

And how do humans avail themselves of his redeeming activity? With these questions, I began my search for answers.

In 1999, my search took on a direction of its own. Looking back, I see that there then began a period which has lasted nearly a decade during which, every time I needed a direction, the necessary book seemed to appear in my hand or the necessary mentor or advisor showed up.

It started in August, 1999, when I went to my local Borders bookstore to buy myself a book for my birthday. I was actually looking for a book by John Henry Newman when my eye strayed to the shelf above, where I saw Hans Küng's book, *Christianity: Essence, History, and Future*. I pulled it down and browsed and saw that it had fascinating endpapers, which diagramed the great historical changes in the Christian churches. So I bought it and devoured it in nine days. Küng's book led me to the works of Friedrich Schleiermacher, a great nineteenth century German theologian who didn't accept the teaching that the death of Jesus was an act of atonement to God for the sins of humanity, and who wrote a massive work of dogmatic theology, *The Christian Faith*, without needing that theory. So I bought and read Schleiermacher's book and learned his theology of God and of the nature of Jesus.

In May, 2000, Garry Wills's book *Papal Sin* was published, and there he briefly described the work of the French scholar René Girard, who maintained that Jesus died not as a sacrifice but in opposition to all sacrifices. I immediately bought and read Girard's principal works, particularly his *Things Hidden Since the Foundation of the World*. Girard's theory of what I call the "culture of sacrifice" is the basis of my discussion in Chapter 3.

I have a good friend and law partner with whom I've enjoyed many lunchtime discussions, talking about my study and writing, and his. In early 2001 he put on my desk Robert Wright's *The Moral Animal*, which introduced me to the naturally selected and genetically based anti-social behaviors of humans, which I discuss in Chapter 2.

Meanwhile, I had started to write down my own thoughts and discoveries. At one point in late 2000, I was trying to find a way to explain in my own words the teachings of Schleiermacher about the nature of Jesus. I awoke in the middle of one night with the idea that I could collect from the Gospel of John all of the sayings of Jesus about his relationship with his Father, and see whether Schleier-macher's explanations were supported and could be illustrated by these sayings. So I got out of bed and started to work, and that approach came out surprisingly well.

Some time later, in 2001, I took on the job of organizing all the sayings of Jesus, so that I could understand more clearly his ethical and other teachings. Buoyed by my success with his teachings about his relationship with his Father, I started dividing and sorting the teachings of Jesus by topic. To my surprise, the ethical teachings of Jesus appeared to be concentrated on five topics, to the almost complete exclusion of a lot of topics which I had expected to find but didn't. At first I called these five ethical topics the "key virtues," as they were certainly key in the thoughts of Jesus. Later on I decided that they could better be called "the five commandments of Jesus," and that they were what Jesus was referring to when he instructed his followers to "keep my commandments." The five commandments of Jesus, and their basis in the words of Jesus, are set forth in Chapter 1.

Over the Labor Day weekend in 2001, I attended a forty-fifth anniversary reunion of the men with whom I had entered the Jesuit order in 1956, the first reunion of that group. A week later, the events of September 11 prompted us all to exchange reactions and feelings. Two months later, a member of the group circulated an address given by James Alison, an English Catholic theologian, at Downside Abbey in England, containing his reflections on September 11. I thus discovered this brilliant Catholic writer and theologian who also rejected the idea that the death of Jesus was a sacrifice, and who wrote as a confirmed follower of René Girard.

And in 2005, I discovered the writings of Roger Haight, S.J., who has since become my mentor and good friend, only because I read in the paper that the Vatican had condemned his major work, *Jesus Symbol of God*, and had banned him from teaching at any Catholic university or seminary. Roger introduced me to the scripture scholarship of John P. Meier, and to the writings of Juan Luis Segundo.

I gradually became aware of, and surprised by, the chain of coincidences which had led me this far on my search for a new approach to Christianity. I had chanced on the book by Küng while I was looking for another book by another author, and Küng led me to Schleiermacher. Wills's *Papal Sin* said almost nothing about the non-sacrificial death of Jesus, but it introduced me to Girard, who does. I had never heard of Wright's *The Moral Animal*, and my law partner who put it on my desk had no idea that it would fill an important gap in my developing approach to the teachings of Jesus. An inspiration in the middle of the night had led me to a close study and organization of the teachings of Jesus, without which I would never have seen his five commandments. The circulation of James Alison's address occasioned by September 11 was fortuitous, and so was the censure of Haight by the Vatican's Holy Office. Both led me to new and sympathetic advisors, mentors, and friends.

I had experienced, it seems, a run of very good luck. When I described this sequence of events to the rector of All Saints Episcopal Church in Hilton Head, South Carolina, where I have found my spiritual home, he asked if I saw the action of the Spirit in this series of coincidences. I'm almost persuaded of that, but I don't want to be presumptuous, and I'm not completely sure. He's confident that the Spirit of God has been supporting my work.

Putting some of this together, it finally dawned on me, or rather hit me like a thunderbolt, that Jesus had directed his five commandments precisely against the genetically based behaviors of humans, both as they manifest themselves in individuals and as they were and are embodied in human institutions within the culture of sacrifice. I now had my "three-legged stool" of commandments, genetically based behaviors, and the culture of sacrifice, and a three-legged stool has stability. This insight, or connection, explains what Jesus was doing, and what he was talking about. It also explains how we, you and I together, can participate in the plan of Jesus for the redemption of humanity, and why we can reasonably hope for ultimate success.

The central finding of this book is that the most important direction of Jesus to his followers, the Christians, is that we accept and practice his five commandments. The central doctrinal conclusion is that this acceptance and practice will lead to the redemption of the world.

This is the new approach to Christianity which I've found, and in which I find peace and hope. It's an approach which will change lives – it may change your life – it has changed mine!

The three-legged stool is set forth in Chapters 1, 2, and 3. The rest of the book works out many important implications of the first three chapters: how this approach replaces the traditional doctrine of original sin, in Chapter 4; how the teachings of Jesus on the kingdom of God and his systematic attacks on the elements of sacrificial culture reinforce and enlarge this approach, in Chapter 5; how the death and resurrection of Jesus confirm this understanding of his mission, in Chapter 6; how the five commandments of Jesus may be applied in our personal lives and to public social, political, and cultural issues and institutions, in Chapters 7 and 8; how and in what way Jesus is both human and divine, in Chapter 9; and how we can go about studying and practicing the five commandments in community with each other, in Chapter 10.

This approach to Christianity through the five commandments of Jesus produces a view of Christianity which is reasonable and practical; not practical in the sense of being easy to practice, which it isn't, but in the sense that it's focused on real-world problems to which it offers difficult but sensible real-world answers. This approach describes a Christianity without magic and superstition, and a Christianity in which humans with their freedom and creativity can and do participate in the redeeming activity of Jesus.

As this approach emphasizes the ethical teachings of Jesus, so it de-emphasizes orthodoxy, or faithful acceptance of the doctrinal and historical teachings of Christian churches. To be sure, there are some central and essential teachings which are part of being a Christian, and I don't abandon them. But as we shall see, in the bulk of his teachings Jesus himself emphasized changing our attitudes and then our conduct, and he said comparatively little about matters of doctrine. So the approach I propose allows for considerable latitude in belief with respect to doctrinal and historical teachings traditionally held by the Christian churches, as for example the miracles of Jesus, or the doctrine of the Trinity, as long as this latitude doesn't affect our acceptance of Jesus's ethical teachings or our attitude or conduct toward our fellow humans.

This isn't to say that I haven't formed views of my own on these and similar issues. Where these questions come up in the course of the book, I'll present my views and my reasons for them. I simply ask you to bear in mind that I have no problem if you take a different view, as long as that view doesn't adversely affect your understanding and practice of the five commandments of Jesus.

As this is more an extended essay than a scholarly work, I haven't used footnotes. Each chapter will be followed with a short appendix called "Notes and Sources for Further Reading," which will give sources for quotations and will cite and sometimes briefly describe the principal works relied on for the material covered. I'll generally use the New Revised Standard Version of the Bible for quotations from the Gospels in this book. I'll occasionally substitute the language of older translations, particularly where they seem more familiar or more comfortable. For example, I'll use "forgive us our trespasses" rather than "forgive us our debts," and "the mote and the beam" rather than "the speck and the log."

After each passage quoted from a Gospel, I'll cite the Gospel in which it is found (abbreviating the writer's name to Mt, Mk, Lk, or Jn), followed by the chapter number and, after the colon, the number of the verse or verses. Where a quoted passage is followed by the citation of two or more scriptural passages, the quoted passage comes from the first of the references, and the other references are to parallel passages in other Gospels.

I'm grateful to my mentor and friend Roger Haight, S.J., who gave me counsel throughout the period of development of this book, and who read and commented on the drafts; to my sisters Ellen Erzen and Martha Zachlin, my nephew Mark Erzen, and my friend Kathy Baker, who read the whole book in various drafts and gave me extended and helpful comments; to other friends and relatives who read parts of various drafts and offered helpful advice; to my friends at All Saints Episcopal Church who participated in the first discussion group on the book and who read and discussed the first draft; to Donald Cutler, who gave me astute advice about trimming and focusing the work; to my friend Charlotte Beck, who gave the final draft a thorough, professional, and very helpful edit; and to my friends Marjorie Milbrandt and Vivian Hughes, who helped me prepare a Discussion and Study Guide to this book, available on the website, Thefivecommandments-ofJesus.com. I'm grateful for the help, patience, and forbearance of my wife Betty throughout the long sessions of drafting and revising the manuscript.

I

DISCOVERING THE FIVE COMMANDMENTS

"If you love me, keep my commandments." (Jn 14:15)

SUPPOSE YOU WANTED to look something up in the Gospels; say, for example, what did Jesus teach about prayer? Would this be difficult or easy? Surprisingly, it can be quite difficult. Some of the teachings of Jesus on prayer are in the Sermon on the Mount, Chapters 5 through 7 of the Gospel of Matthew (always a good place to start): Mt 6:5-15, 7:7-11. But the rest, and some important ones, are scattered throughout the Gospels in no particular order. I found that this is true of nearly all of the teachings of Jesus.

Suppose you wanted to find, as I wanted to find, a plan or a central organizing theme in the teachings, particularly the ethical teachings, of Jesus? Unless you do the sorting and listing exercise I describe below, you almost certainly won't find one; until I did this exercise myself, I couldn't see one.

So I looked more closely at the Gospels. What I found was that the sayings and sermons of Jesus jump from one topic to another with no apparent plan or connection. Teachings on the same subject are scattered here and there. Some teachings are set forth in a single saying, never repeated. Others are repeated in various forms in different places, but the Gospel writers only occasionally brought them together. Read the Sermon on the Mount again, and I think you'll see what I mean.

How did this come about? I asked myself. I began to imagine the way the writers of the Gospels had assembled their materials. I imagined a fellow with a pad of papyrus and a large leather backpack, going from one person who had heard Jesus speak to another who had written down what he remembered Jesus to have said. "What did Jesus say?" the seeker would ask. Then he'd write down the remembered words, or copy the written record or memorandum of the words of Jesus kept by the person he was questioning, on a piece of papyrus, and stuff it into his backpack. After he'd done this for a while, he'd go back to his home or his tent, get them all out, and sort them – sayings here, miracles there, parables in a third pile. He didn't think it was his job to impose an order on the sayings. Well, perhaps the writer of the Gospel of John did. The first three Gospels are more disorganized.

This troubled me. I have an organized mind (a prerequisite for a practicing lawyer), so I started making lists, sorting, and organizing the sayings of Jesus by subject matter. To my surprise, there began to appear certain ethical teachings of Jesus which he repeated over and over, sometimes in command, sometimes in metaphor, sometimes in warning, sometimes in parable. In particular, I was able to identify five rules of ethical conduct which stood out from the rest. This is the genesis of what I call the five commandments of Jesus.

I also discovered from this exercise that Jesus gave much greater importance to his teaching activities than we usually give to them. He said that his teaching was what he came to do, and that salvation would come from his teaching. Jesus said,

> I must proclaim the good news of the kingdom of God to the other cities also, for *I was sent for this purpose.* (Lk 4:43)

> For this I was born, and for this I came into the world, to testify to the truth. (Jn 18:37)

> The words that I have spoken to you are spirit and life. (Jn 6:63)

> If you continue in my word, you are truly my disciples; and you will know the truth, and the truth will make you free. (Jn 8:31-32)

> Whoever keeps my word will never see death. (Jn 8:51)

In Jesus's own words, his teaching activity is why he was born and what he was sent to do, and those who accept his teachings and follow them will live forever. This makes his teachings very important indeed.

Many of the teachings of Jesus are ethical teachings. He some-times called them his "commandments" and at other times called them his "word." He spoke repeatedly about the importance of keeping his commandments (or his "words") in his Last Supper discourse to his disciples, Chapters 14 -17 of John's Gospel:

> If you love me, keep my commandments. (Jn 14:15)

> Those who have my commandments and keep them are those who love me; and those who love me will be loved by my

Father, and I will love them and reveal myself to them. (Jn 14:21)

Those who love me will keep my word, and my Father will love them, and we will come to them and make our abode with them. Whoever does not love me does not keep my words. (Jn 14:23-24)

If you abide in me, and my words abide in you, ask for whatever you wish, and it will be done for you. (Jn 15:7)

If you keep my commandments, you will abide in my love, just as I have kept my Father's commandments and abide in his love. (Jn 15:10)

You are my friends if you do what I command you. (Jn 15:14)

I am giving you these commands so that you may love one another. (Jn 15:17)

Some Scripture scholars are uncomfortable with relying on sayings of Jesus which appear only in the Gospel of John, because John's Gospel appears to be so carefully composed and so different from the other Gospels. But the Last Supper discourse wasn't the first or the only time Jesus spoke of the importance of keeping his commandments. In the middle of the Sermon on the Mount, which contains many commandments of Jesus, he said:

Whoever breaks one of the least of these commandments, and teaches others to do the same, will be called least in the kingdom of heaven; but whoever does them and teaches them will be called great in the kingdom of heaven. (Mt 5:19)

Generally, when Jesus taught an important teaching, he illustrated it with a memorable metaphor or parable. So he did with this teaching, at the conclusion of the Sermon on the Mount:

Everyone then who hears these words of mine and acts on them will be like a wise man who built his house on rock. The rain fell, the floods came, and the winds blew and beat on that house, but it did not fall, because it had been founded on rock. And everyone who hears these words of mine and does not act on them will be like a foolish man who built his house on sand. The rain fell, and the floods came, and the winds blew and beat against that house, and it fell – and great was its fall! (Mt 7:24-27; Lk 6:47-49)

When on one occasion the crowd told him that his mother and his brothers were waiting outside, he replied, "My mother and my brothers are those who hear the word of God and do it" (Lk 8:21; Mk 3:33-35; Mt 12:49-50). And this teaching was part of the great commission given by Jesus to his disciples:

> Go therefore and make disciples of all nations, baptizing them in the name of the Father and of the Son and of the Holy Spirit, *and teaching them to obey everything that I have commanded you.* (Mt 28:19-20)

This repeated demand that people keep his commandments is as clear and insistent as anything Jesus said. According to this teaching, we could hardly pretend to be Christians without trying to obey the commandments of Jesus. But what are those commandments? I found I didn't know what they are.

We'd expect that the Christian churches would teach and preach the commandments of Jesus as a prominent part of their mission. But they don't. We'd expect at least that there would be a list of the commandments of Jesus, available to the faithful on request. There isn't. It's easy to find a list of the ten commandments of Moses in any church or courthouse in the country (in courthouses thanks not to the Christian right but to C. B. DeMille). There are lists of the seven deadly sins, the four cardinal virtues, the fifteen (or is it twenty now?) mysteries of the rosary, and so forth, but no list of the commandments of Jesus.

In a random and unscientific survey, I asked a number of friends and relatives, all good Christians, if they knew the commandments of Jesus. Nearly all were puzzled by the question. It had never occurred to them that there should be a list of the commandments of Jesus. Most of those who ventured an answer said that what must be meant by the commandments of Jesus is what Episcopalians call the Summary of the Law: Love the Lord your God with all your heart, etc., and Love your neighbor as yourself. Several also suggested that Jesus gave us a single commandment, that we love one another.

That's what's set forth in the Catechism in the Episcopal Church's Book of Common Prayer, p. 851:

Q. What response did Christ require?

A.   Christ commanded us to believe in him and to keep his commandments.

Q.   What are the commandments taught by Christ?
A.   Christ taught us the Summary of the Law and gave us the New Commandment.

Q.   What is the Summary of the Law?
A.   You shall love the Lord your God with all your heart, with all your soul, and with all your mind. This is the first and the great commandment. And the second is like it: You shall love your neighbor as yourself.

Q.   What is the New Commandment?
A.   The New Commandment is that we love one another as Christ loved us.

I think this is almost entirely wrong. Jesus didn't teach the Summary of the Law. The Summary of the Law is found only once in the Gospels. (Scripture scholars treat episodes in the Gospel of Mark which are repeated in Matthew and Luke as having one source, not three.) In an episode found in Mark, Matthew, and Luke (Mt 22:34-40; Mk 12:28-34; Lk 10:25-28), a scribe or lawyer asked Jesus a question to test him. Matthew puts the question as "Teacher, which commandment in the law is the greatest?" Mark puts the question in similar words. Luke puts it as "Teacher, what must I do to inherit eternal life?" In answer to the question in Matthew and in Mark, Jesus recited the Summary of the Law. In Luke, Jesus responded with a question of his own: "What is written in the law? What do you read there?" The lawyer recited the Summary of the Law, and Jesus approved the answer.

There's thus an initial uncertainty: did Jesus himself ever actually recite the Summary of the Law himself, or did he simply listen to its recitation by the lawyer? Did Luke change the story by adding an error, or did he correct an error made by Mark and copied by Matthew? Of course, even if Jesus did recite the Summary of the Law, he didn't "teach" it. Answering a test question isn't the same as teaching. And there's no doubt that Jesus clearly identified the Summary of the Law as commandments of the "Law," which is to say of the Torah, the first five books of the Hebrew Scriptures. The two great commandments are in fact set forth at Deuteronomy 6:5 and Leviticus 19:18. Jesus wouldn't have identified commandments from the Hebrew Scriptures as "my" commandments.

The New Commandment, that we love one another, is similarly unlikely as a candidate for one of the commandments of Jesus. It was first taught as a commandment in Jesus's Last Supper discourse, at John 13:34 and 15:17, rather late for a principal teaching. And "Love one another" is simply another way of expressing the second great commandment, that we must love our neighbor as ourselves. It's not an original teaching of Jesus. While the command to love one another summarizes and underlies all of the ethical teachings of Jesus, it's not itself new.

A second problem with the New Commandment as well as with the Summary of the Law is that both of them are on a level of generality unsuitable for a commandment. Love, that strange and highly personal combination of emotion, desire, self-deception, and choice, is a powerful motivation but an unreliable guide to conduct. What we should be looking for in the teachings of Jesus are commandments like the ten commandments of Moses: commands to do or to avoid doing a specific kind of moral act or practice. The New Commandment and the second great commandment, however noble, don't tell me anything specific about what I must do and what I must avoid, in the way that "Thou shalt not steal" and "Thou shalt not kill" are specific. The lawyer who questioned Jesus about the Summary of the Law didn't know to whom the command to love one's neighbor should be applied, let alone how (Lk 10:29). So he asked Jesus, "Who is my neighbor?" Jesus responded by telling the parable of the Good Samaritan. We'll be able to find teachings of Jesus which tell us specifically what we must do and what we must avoid. We should look to these teachings for his commandments.

A third problem with the Summary of the Law and the New Commandment is that they're singularly unhelpful guides to the conduct of groups and institutions. A nation or a political party may, for example, adopt a policy of nonviolence, or of equality between persons, but neither a nation nor a party can adopt love as a policy or program. Neither the Summary of the Law nor the New Commandment address communal or social sin.

It can of course be suggested that all of the teachings of Jesus are important, and that a listing of selected commandments is unnecessary and will leave out important teachings. But Jesus himself indicated that he thought that some of his ethical teachings were more important than others, because he repeated the more important ones many times and illustrated them with metaphor and parable. We ought to identify these teachings if we can. The absence of a list of the commandments of Jesus leads to an absence of focus on what Jesus actually taught. A listing will shed light on what Jesus considered to be his core teachings and the center of his ethical revelation.

So I decided to sort and organize the ethical teachings of Jesus, so that I could identify his commandments. The principles of sorting and selection I developed and used are these four rules:

First, a commandment of Jesus should be an original ethical teaching of Jesus, new and different from the teachings of the Hebrew Scriptures or those of any other ethical tradition of ancient times. When Jesus says "You have heard that it was said to those of ancient times . . . But I say to you . . .", this is a clue that Jesus is claiming, and delivering, a new and original ethical teaching. For this reason, among others, I don't consider the care of the poor, important as it is, to be among the commandments of Jesus, for it's not an original teaching. In contrast, non-judging, forgiveness, nonviolence, humility, and detachment from possessions aren't taught in the Torah, nor with any consistency in the rest of the Hebrew Scriptures. They are original teachings of Jesus.

Second, Jesus repeated some of his ethical teachings over and over, often in different circumstances and in different words, and these repetitions are found in many different Gospel sources. The emphasis which Jesus thus gave to these teachings indicates strongly that they are among his commandments.

Third, Jesus wanted his commandments to be understood and remembered. It's a strong indication that an ethical teaching of Jesus is among his commandments if Jesus taught it both by direct instruction and in a memorable illustration, metaphor, or parable. All of the commandments set forth below are supported not only by texts of direct command but also by one or more vivid metaphors or parables.

Fourth and finally, it's generally true that the sermon or lecture, the "stump speech," contains the message the speaker came to convey. The answers a speaker gives to questions asked during the question-and-answer period may be important, but they address topics selected by the questioner, not the speaker, and they may or may not be what the speaker considers important. For example, the statement of Jesus about the indissolubility of marriage, "What God has joined together, let no man put asunder" (Mt 19:6; Mk 10:9), was given in answer to a test question from the Pharisees and isn't central to his message. I give greater importance to the teachings of Jesus which appear in his direct preaching than I do to the material he covered in the Q-and-A periods.

With these selection criteria in mind, I sorted the ethical teachings of Jesus by subject. I didn't select the subjects; Jesus (with the help of the gospel writers, and their leather backpacks) selected the subjects. Whatever the subject matter, if the ethical teaching was original with Jesus, frequently repeated, memorably illustrated, and set forth in his direct preaching, it made the list.

Five, and only five, ethical teachings or commandments of Jesus emerged from this study. Nothing else in all of the ethical teachings of Jesus approaches these five commandments in originality, frequency, and force of expression. What follows is a list of these five commandments of Jesus. I've summarized each commandment in my own words, to try to collate into one short sentence the several teachings of Jesus on each subject, and I've followed each statement of a commandment with quotations from the teachings of Jesus which support, explain, illustrate, and elaborate that commandment.

I. Do Not Judge, Blame, Condemn, or Exclude
Any Person From Your Fellowship and Love.

Do not judge, so that you may not be judged. For with the judgment you make you will be judged, and the measure you give will be the measure you get. Why do you see the mote in your neighbor's eye, but do not see the beam in your own eye? Or how can you say to your neighbor, "Let me take the mote out of your eye," while the beam is in your own eye? You hypocrite, first take the beam out of your own eye, and then you will see clearly to take the mote out of your neighbor's eye. (Mt 7:1-5; Lk 6:37-38, 41-42)

You have heard that it was said, "You shall love your neighbor and hate your enemy." But I say to you, Love your enemies and pray for those that persecute you, so that you may be children of your Father in heaven; for he makes his sun rise on the evil and on the good, and sends rain on the righteous and on the unrighteous. For if you love those who love you, what reward do you have? Do not even the tax collectors do the same? And if you greet only your brothers and sisters, what more are you doing than others? Do not even the Gentiles do the same? Be perfect, therefore, as your heavenly Father is perfect. (Mt 5:43-48; Lk 6:27-28, 32-36)

Let the one among you who is without sin be the first to throw a stone at her. (Jn 8:7)

Jesus replied, "A man was going down from Jerusalem to Jericho, and fell into the hands of robbers, who stripped him, beat him, and went away, leaving him half dead. Now by chance a priest was going down that road; and when he saw him, he passed by on the other side. So likewise a Levite, when he came to the place and saw him, passed by on the other side. But a Samaritan while traveling came near him; and when he saw him, he was moved with pity. He went to him and bandaged his wounds, having poured oil and wine on them. Then he put him on his own animal, brought him to an inn, and took care of him. The next day he took out two denarii, gave them to the innkeeper, and said, 'Take care of him; and when I come back, I will repay you whatever more you spend.' Which of these three, do you think, was a neighbor to the man who fell into the hands of the robbers?" He said, "The one who showed him mercy." Jesus said to him, "Go and do likewise." (Lk 10:30-37)

It's important to know that the Greek word in Matthew 7:1 and Luke 6:37 translated as "judge," *krinete*, means "judge" as in pass judgment on, blame, condemn, or exclude. That's why my paraphrase of this teaching of Jesus is somewhat extended. In Luke's version, Jesus expands his teaching on non-judging to make this clear, and then closely links non-judging with forgiveness: "Do not judge, and you will not be judged. Do not condemn, and you will not be condemned. Forgive, and you will be forgiven" (Lk 6:37). To "judge" thus means not only to find fault in another, but also to blame, condemn, or exclude that person for that fault. It means to make another person the enemy, the one worthy of blame, exclusion, and punishment. So the scribes and Pharisees had "judged" the woman caught in adultery and were ready to stone her to death (Jn 8:2-11).

"Judging" is frequently a social or communal sin; that is, it's practiced by a group acting as one. It's in this form that it does its greatest harm. Class, ethnic, national, and religious differences become toxic when they result, as they often do, in "judging," where members of one class, ethnic group, nation, or religion decide that the "other" is the enemy, worthy of blame, exclusion, condemnation, and often violence.

"Judging" has a particular relationship to violence, especially retaliatory violence. As a rule, we can't inflict violence on another without first excluding him or her from our own group and treating him or her as the enemy, or as a criminal, undeserving of the right of every person to our respect, fellowship, and love. This means that if we truly refrain from judging we will be nonviolent as well.

Jesus illustrated this teaching in two ways in the story of the Good Samaritan. The priest and the Levite who passed by the injured Jew apparently "judged" him to be of a lower or "other" class, and excluded him from their duty to help. The Samaritan, who was of an ethnic group excluded by the Jews, didn't "judge" the injured Jew but instead gave him the aid which was needed.

Jesus lived his rule of welcoming and loving people of all excluded groups. He was regularly reproached by the scribes and Pharisees for being "a friend of tax collectors and sinners" (*e.g.,* Lk 7:34). On one occasion a local woman, known as a "sinner," entered the house of a Pharisee who had invited Jesus to dinner and anointed Jesus's feet with ointment and her tears. Jesus vigorously defended her, illustrated his point with a parable, and forgave her her sins (Lk 7:36-50). In Jesus's time, tax collectors, or tax farmers, who used to be called "publicans" in older translations, were assumed, usually with good reason, to be dishonest, or disloyal to Israel, or both. Jesus called Matthew (also called Levi), a tax collector, to be one of his disciples (Mt 9:9; Mk 2:13-17; Lk 5:27-28). And Jesus scandalized the righteous when he singled out Zacchaeus, a rich tax collector, to be his host at Jericho (Lk 19:1-10).

II. FORGIVE ALL WHO HAVE OFFENDED YOU.

Forgive us our trespasses, as we forgive those who trespass against us. (Mt 6:12; Lk 11:4)

For if you forgive others their trespasses, your heavenly Father will also forgive you; but if you do not forgive others, neither will your heavenly Father forgive your trespasses. (Mt 6:14-15; Mk 11:25-26; Lk 6:37)

Then Peter came and said to him, "Lord, if my brother sins against me, how often should I forgive? As many as seven times?" Jesus said to him, "Not seven times, but, I tell you, seventy times seven times." (Mt 18:21-22; Lk 17:3-4)

Jesus immediately followed this teaching (in Matthew) with the parable of the unjust debtor. After the king had forgiven the debtor his huge debt to the king, the debtor refused to forgive a small debt of another servant to him. The king severely punished the debtor for this act (Mt. 18:23-35).

In the parable of the prodigal son (Lk 15:11-32), Jesus taught that the Father rejoices in forgiving the repentant sinner. Jesus forgave the sins of a paralytic man who was brought to him for healing and then healed him (Mk 2:1-12; Mt 9:2-8; Lk 5:17-26). He forgave the sins of the woman who bathed his feet with her tears (Lk 7:36-50). And from the cross Jesus forgave his executioners, saying, "Father, forgive them, for they know not what they do" (Lk 23:34).

It's quite rare to find Jesus teaching that the judgment of God on any person will be conditioned upon that person's obedience to a particular commandment. He did so in the case of the commandments of non-judging and forgiveness:

Do not judge, so that you may not be judged. For with the judgment you make you will be judged, and the measure you give will be the measure you get. (Mt 7:1-2)

For if you forgive others their trespasses, your heavenly Father will also forgive you; but if you do not forgive others, neither will your heavenly Father forgive your trespasses. (Mt 6:14-15; Mk 11:25-26; Lk 6:37)

This is a good indication of how important Jesus thought these two commandments are. No other ethical teachings of Jesus are accompanied by such a severe warning of the consequences of failure.

III. Do Not Do Violence to Any Person, Even in Response to Violence.

You have heard that it was said, "An eye for an eye and a tooth for a tooth." But I say to you, do not resist an evildoer. If anyone strikes you on the right cheek, turn the other also; and if anyone wants to sue you and take your coat, give your cloak as well; and if anyone forces you to go one mile, go also the second mile. (Mt 5:38-41; Lk 6:29)

You have heard that it was said, "You shall love your neighbor and hate your enemy." But I say to you, Love your enemies and pray for those who persecute you. (Mt 5:43-44; Lk 6:27-28)

Blessed are the peacemakers, for they will be called children of God. (Mt 5:9)

You have heard it was said to those of ancient times, "You shall not murder;" and "whoever murders shall be liable to judgment." But I say to you that if you are angry with a brother or sister, you will be liable to judgment; and if you insult a brother or sister, you will be liable to the council; and if you say, "You fool," you will be liable to the hell of fire. (Mt 5:21-22)

Suddenly, one of those with Jesus put his hand on his sword, drew it, and struck the servant of the high priest, cutting off his ear. Then Jesus said to him, "Put your sword back into its place; for all who take the sword will perish by the sword." (Mt 26:51-52; Lk 22:50-51; Jn 18:10-11)

The American theologian Walter Wink has pointed out that the Greek phrase which is translated "do not resist an evildoer" actually means "do not *use violence to* resist an evildoer." Active nonviolent resistance to the violence of another is what Jesus taught, and this is reflected in my paraphrase of the teaching.

The commandment of Jesus not to do violence, even in response to violence, has been ignored by many Christians and many Christian nations throughout the history of Christianity. Nonviolence is closely related to the commandments of non-judging and forgiveness; the three act together. If we are followers of the teachings of Jesus, we repress the urge to retaliate with violence for an insult or injury. We make allowance for the fault of the person giving the injury, reflect on the beam in our own eye, and withdraw our adverse judgment of that person. Then we put the matter at peace within ourselves and put it behind us when we forgive the other person.

IV. Act as a Humble Servant Toward All Others.

The kings of the Gentiles lord it over them, and those in authority over them are called benefactors. But not so with you; rather the greatest among you must become like the youngest, and the leader like one who serves. For who is greater, the one who is at table or the one who serves? Is it not the one at the table? But I am among you as one who serves. (Lk 22:25-27; Mt 20:25-28; Mk 10:42-45)

But you are not to be called rabbi, for you have one teacher and you are all students. And call no one your father on earth, for you have one Father – the one in heaven. Nor are you to be called instructors, for you have one instructor, the Messiah. The greatest among you will be your servant. All who exalt themselves will be humbled, and all who humble themselves will be exalted. (Mt 23:8-12)

When you are invited by someone to a wedding banquet, do not sit down at the place of honor, lest someone more distinguished than you has been invited by your host; and the host who invited both of you may come and say to you, "Give this person your place," and then in disgrace you would start to take the lowest place. But when you are invited, go and sit down at the lowest place, so that when your host comes, he may say to you, "Friend, move up higher"; then you will be honored in the presence of all who sit at the table with you. For all who exalt themselves will be humbled, and those who humble themselves will be exalted. (Lk 14:8-11)

Who among you would say to your servant who has just come in from plowing or tending sheep in the field, "Come here at once and take your place at the table"? Would you not rather say to him, "Prepare supper for me, put on your apron and serve me while I eat and drink; later you may eat and drink"? Do you thank the servant for doing what was commanded? So you also, when you have done all that you were ordered to do, say, "We are unworthy servants; we have done only what we ought to have done!" (Lk 17:7-10)

He also told this parable to some who trusted in themselves that they were righteous and regarded others with contempt: "Two men went up to the temple to pray, one a Pharisee and the other a tax collector. The Pharisee, standing by himself, was praying thus, 'God, I thank you that I am not like other people: thieves, rogues, adulterers, or even like this tax collector. I fast twice a week; I give a tenth of all my income.' But the tax collector, standing far off, would not even look up to heaven, but was beating his breast and saying, 'God, be merciful to me, a sinner!' I tell you, this man went down to his home justified rather than the other; for all who exalt themselves will be humbled, but all who humble themselves will be exalted." (Lk 18:9-14)

Jesus taught that every person is beloved of God, and thus that all persons are equal in God's sight:

Which one of you, having a hundred sheep and losing one of them, does not leave the ninety-nine in the wilderness and go after the one that is lost until he finds it? When he has found it, he lays it on his shoulders and rejoices. And when he comes home, he calls together his friends and neighbors, saying to them, "Rejoice with me, for I have found my sheep that was lost." Just so, I tell you, there will be more joy in heaven over one sinner who repents than over ninety-nine righteous persons who need no repentance. (Lk 15:3-7; Mt 18:12-14)

And at the Last Supper Jesus washed the feet of his disciples (Jn 13:3-16).

In this group of teachings, Jesus combined two closely-related but distinct ideas: first, the idea of the fundamental equality of all human persons, which undercuts any justification for dominant-submissive relationships, or for putting on airs; and second, the idea of service, in which the model for action is to help others, not to rule them. As these ideas are intertwined in the teachings of Jesus, I've combined them in the phrase "humble servant."

Jesus is too good a psychologist to command that each person should consider himself equal to everyone else. To counter the universal and persistent human desire to feel superior, he commanded that each person act humbly toward others. His astute insight into human psychology counsels us to use our very desire to win praise and avoid humiliation to develop the habit of acting humbly, as when one takes the lower place at table.

V. DETACH YOURSELF FROM POSSESSIONS.

Do not store up for yourselves treasures on earth, where moth and rust consume and where thieves break in and steal; but store up for yourselves treasures in heaven, where neither moth nor rust consumes and where thieves do not break in and steal. For where your treasure is, there your heart will be also. (Mt 6:19-21; Lk 12:33-34)

No one can serve two masters. Either he will hate the one and love the other, or he will be devoted to the one and despise the other. You cannot serve both God and money. (Mt 6:24; Lk 16:13)

Therefore I tell you, do not worry about your life, what you will eat or drink, or about your body, what you will wear. Is not life more than food, and the body more than clothing? Look at the birds of the air; they neither sow nor reap nor gather into barns, and yet your heavenly Father feeds them. Are you not of more value than they? And can any of you by worrying add a single hour to your span of life? And why do you worry about clothing? Consider the lilies of the field, how they grow; they neither toil nor spin, yet I tell you, even Solomon in all his glory was not clothed like one of these. But if God so clothes the grass of the field, which is alive today and tomorrow is thrown into the oven, will he not much more clothe you – you of little faith? Therefore do not worry, saying, "What will we eat?" or "What will we drink?" or "What will we wear?" For it is the Gentiles who strive for all these things; and indeed your heavenly Father knows that you need all these things. But strive first for the kingdom of God and his righteousness, and all these things will be given to you as well. (Mt 6:25-33; Lk12:22-31)

Truly I tell you, it will be hard for a rich man to enter the kingdom of heaven. Again I tell you, it is easier for a camel to go through the eye of a needle than for a rich man to enter the kingdom of God. (Mt 19:23-24; Mk 10:23-25; Lk 18:24-25)

And he said to them, "Take care! Be on your guard against all kinds of greed; for one's life does not consist in the abundance of possessions." Then he told them a parable: "The land of a rich man produced abundantly. And he thought to himself, 'What shall I do, for I have no place to store my crops?' Then he said, 'I will do this: I will pull down my barns and build larger ones, and there I will store all my grain and my goods. And I will say to my soul, Soul, you have ample goods laid up for many years; relax, eat, drink, be merry.' But God said to him, 'You fool! This very night your life is being demanded of you. And the things you have prepared, whose will they be?' So it is with those who store up riches for themselves but are not rich in what matters to God." (Lk 12:15-21)

Jesus didn't counsel poverty, or living apart from the world, except to a very few. As I'll develop later, the principal mission of his followers is to be in the world, to change it. This requires both money and possessions and prudent management of them. Jesus simply insisted that we get and keep our priorities straight. In addition to the duty to develop personal detachment from possessions, this commandment implies a duty to strive for economic justice and for the alleviation of poverty, for as a practical matter a person in abject poverty can't cease to worry about food, drink, clothing, and shelter until basic subsistence is reliably available.

*   *   *   *   *

These, I submit, are the five commandments of Jesus. There's only one other command or direction of Jesus which he repeated over and over and illustrated with metaphor and parable, and that's his instruction to pray to the Father privately, persistently, frequently, and with confidence. I haven't classified it with the five commandments for two reasons: first, because it doesn't directly bear on our ethical obligations toward other people; and second, because it seems to me that a primary purpose of prayer is to focus our strength and courage on, and thus support, our observance of the five commandments.

The five commandments of Jesus have several important characteristics in common:

First, they're very hard to practice. They're much more difficult to live by than the "second tablet" commandments of Moses (those which include and follow "Honor thy father and mother"). Nearly all human societies have adopted the rules found in these commandments of Moses (and in the foundational documents of many other cultures) as part of their civil law. A human society can't survive or function without laws requiring filial piety and forbidding murder, stealing, adultery, and giving false witness. In contrast, human societies don't in general respect or support non-judging, forgiveness, nonviolence, humble service, or detachment from possessions. And each of the five commandments of Jesus directs us to resist and act against a primal, ingrained, and to a large extent genetically based inclination in each of us (more on this in the next chapter).

Second, each of the five commandments requires compliance not only in our own personal lives and conduct but also in our communal or group conduct. The commandment not to judge forbids inter-ethnic, inter-national, and inter-religious condemnations, hatreds, and fears not only between individuals but also between communities and societies. The commandment to forgive shows how we are to deal both individually and as a society with real offenses from others. The commandment to avoid violence speaks not only against private violence but also against the communal violence of war and of our criminal justice systems, and shows what's required to attain and preserve peace between individuals and among nations. The commandments of humble service and detachment from possessions speak not only to our personal lives but also against the injustices in our social, political, and economic systems.

Third, the five commandments are closely interrelated. Non-judging and forgiveness are necessary preconditions to the practice of nonviolence, and so are the attitudes of humble service and detachment from possessions. It's only with humility that we can approach and understand the duty not to judge.

* * * * *

These five commandments are based on teachings of Jesus found in the Gospels. But can we be sure that Jesus actually did teach these particular teachings? Some people believe that we can't be reasonably sure. This uncertainty arises partly because the Gospels in their final forms were first circulated, scholars think, between 70 A.D. and 100 A.D., forty to seventy years after the death of Jesus. And many people aren't aware of the power and accuracy of oral memory in a largely illiterate population where people are trained from an early age to remember exactly what they have heard, because they can't rely on written records. Think of the young students in an Islamic madrasa, who are required to memorize the whole Qur'an.

Scripture scholars generally agree that the Gospels contain five separate traditions or sources of sayings and episodes about Jesus: Mark, including the episodes in Mark which are repeated in Matthew and Luke; "Q," which is a body of sayings of Jesus found in both Matthew and Luke but not in Mark; episodes found only in Matthew; episodes found only in Luke; and the Gospel of John. If a saying or teaching of Jesus is found in several different sources, it's more likely to be true to the words of Jesus, because it very likely goes back to the time before the traditions separated. All five of the commandments of Jesus here set forth are supported by sayings found in at least three of the five sources. All five commandments are supported both by sayings of direct command and by metaphor or parable, another indication of authenticity used by scholars.

A third test used by scholars is what they call "discontinuity": that is, the teaching isn't found in the Hebrew Scriptures or in early Christian writings. That's the case with the five commandments. None of them were clearly taught in the Hebrew Scriptures, and the first three at least were contrary to Jewish tradition. The teachings of the five commandments were never quoted and only rarely referred to in the rest of the New Testament or in other early Christian writings. There are other technical criteria used by Scripture scholars generally which also give high probability to the authenticity of the five commandments.

I add what seems to me to be a very good principle of authentication not in the standard list: the test of imaginative illustration. Many of the most memorable images, metaphors, and parables in the Gospels support the five commandments of Jesus: the mote and the beam, turn the other cheek, all who take the sword will perish by the sword, the birds of the air, the lilies of the field, the eye of the needle, the Good Samaritan, the Prodigal Son, and so forth. The presence of this marvelous capacity for imaginative illustration is to me a compelling indication that these words are the authentic words of Jesus.

The writer called Luke wrote the Acts of the Apostles as well as his Gospel. The Gospel of Luke contains some of the great parables of Jesus: the Good Samaritan, the Prodigal Son, Lazarus and Dives, the Pharisee and the Publican. But there are no parables in Acts. Luke apparently couldn't compose them. The three epistles of John were written by the author of the Gospel of John or by his close associates. The Gospel of John is full of extended metaphors Jesus used to describe himself: "I am the bread of life." "I am the light of the world." "I am the good shepherd." "I am the gate for the sheep." "I am the resurrection and the life." "I am the vine, you are the branches." But the three epistles of John contain only one extended metaphor, "God is light." Paul uses metaphors but no stories or parables.

Jesus is the preeminent imaginative literary genius in the New Testament. The metaphors and parables which illustrate his five commandments are unique to him. Any suggestion that the imaginative illustrations of this body of teaching could have been composed one or two generations after the death of Jesus by different writers in response to the needs of their various local Christian communities is ludicrous. One can no more believe that than believe that a committee of Jacobean writers sat down in 1620 and composed the eighteen Shakespeare plays which appeared in print for the first time in the First Folio in 1623. Works of literary genius can't be composed by a committee or by a community.

I've therefore concluded that as a historical matter, based on the application of common sense and of generally-accepted rules of scriptural scholarship, the five commandments of Jesus are his authentic teachings. There are some Christians who would accept this but would say that their conclusion is based on faith, even a "leap of faith," not on reasoned study and analysis. I don't think this is right. Faith involves a person's fundamental views about the purpose and meaning of life, including what you believe about God. Accepting for yourself, and committing to live in accordance with, the five commandments would be a judgment of faith, because it involves your fundamental views of the meaning and purpose of life. But simply accepting as historical fact that Jesus was an early first-century Jewish teacher and preacher, and that he taught the substance of his five commandments, is a conclusion of history, not of faith. It's like the reasonable historical conclusions we make in accepting that Julius Caesar wrote *The Gallic Wars* or that Virgil wrote *The Aeneid*.

But what of the other ethical teachings of Jesus? Aren't they of equal importance? Let's take a look. Surprisingly, there are very few other ethical teachings of Jesus.

I've already discussed the Two Great Commandments and the New Commandment. There's also the Golden Rule, "Do to others as you would have them do to you," a "Q" saying found at Matthew 7:12 and Luke 6:31. While these are important sayings, they aren't new, as they all appear in the Hebrew Scriptures; they each have only one source in the Gospels; and they're at a level of generality which makes them comparatively useless as guides to conduct, particularly conduct of groups and institutions. All three are generalizations quite compatible with the five commandments, but they take on flesh and detail only through the particular instructions of the five commandments.

Two sayings from the Sermon on the Mount, the evil of lusting after a woman, Matthew 5:27-28, and the injunction against taking oaths, Matthew 5:33-37, appear only in Matthew, and their teachings are never repeated. Jesus condemned giving scandal to children in Mark 9:42 and the parallel passages in Matthew and Luke (Mt 18:6-7; Lk 17:1-2), which amounts to one source. And he forbade divorce in Matthew 5:32 and Luke 16:18, a "Q" saying, and in an answer to a question from the Pharisees in Mark 10:2-12 and Matthew 19:3-9.

Several friends have reproached me for leaving out the teachings of Jesus about caring for the poor and assuring that they have food, clothing, and shelter. The reason I've left that body of teaching out is that I can't find it in the Gospels. The admonitions of Jesus to feed the hungry, clothe the naked, visit the imprisoned, and so forth, appear only in the parable of the Last Judgment, which appears in Matthew 25:31-46, and are not repeated in any other Gospel. Jesus did tell the rich young man, "If you wish to be perfect, go, sell your possessions, and give the money to the poor, and you will have treasure in heaven; and come, follow me" (Mk 19:21; Mk 10:21; Lk 18:22). But this is a call to one man to practice poverty, and the poor are incidental. Jesus could even go the other way on this question. When a woman anointed Jesus's head with an expensive ointment, his disciples grumbled that "this ointment could have been sold for a large sum, and the money given to the poor." Jesus disagreed, saying, "You always have the poor with you, but you will not always have me" (Mt 26:6-13; Mk 14:3-9).

But, as I pointed out above, the fifth commandment of Jesus, *Detach yourselves from possessions*, implies a duty to seek economic justice and the alleviation of poverty, so as to free the poor to seek the kingdom of God. Caring for the poor is in the teachings of Jesus, but primarily through his teaching of his fifth commandment.

Another friend asked about the teaching of Jesus that we should seek forgiveness for our sins. The only teaching on that point is in the Lord's Prayer: "Forgive us our trespasses" (Lk 11:4; Mt 6:12). No one ever asked Jesus for forgiveness of sins, nor did he ever tell anyone to seek forgiveness from another, unless that is implied in Matthew 5:23-25. We sometimes think that Jesus taught things he didn't actually teach. The Gospels show that he really concentrated his ethical teachings to a remarkable degree on his five commandments.

So far, I've only identified the five commandments of Jesus. I've yet to draw out their implications, to address how they work in personal and in public life, and to show their relevance to the present situation of humanity and the world. In due course, I'll address these topics and arrive at the present day. But first, our route takes an interesting path through some of the fields and forests of evolutionary psychology and cultural anthropology, a path which sheds surprising light on the scope and purpose of the five commandments of Jesus.

Notes and Sources for Further Reading

Walter Wink's reading of the passage from Matthew on nonviolence is found in *Engaging the Powers* (Fortress Press, 1992), pp. 175-89, a marvelous and important book.

A discussion of the authentication criteria used by New Testament Scripture scholars can be found in Meier, John P., *A Marginal Jew* (Anchor Bible Reference Library), Volume I, *The Roots of the Problem and the Person* (1991), pp.167-195.

The Five Commandments of Jesus

I. Do not judge, blame, condemn, or exclude any person from your fellowship and love.

II. Forgive all who have offended you.

III. Do not do violence to any person, even in response to violence.

IV. Act as a humble servant toward all others.

V. Detach yourself from possessions.

II

EVOLUTIONARY PSYCHOLOGY

*"The world cannot hate you, but it hates me, because
I testify to it that its works are evil" (Jn 7:7)*

ARE THE FIVE COMMANDMENTS OF JESUS a random selection of directives difficult to practice? Or are they a unified, carefully thought out, and carefully crafted solution to the most fundamental problems of humanity? When I first discovered the five commandments, hiding there in plain sight, I called them the key virtues, because they were clearly central, or key, to the body of ethical teachings of Jesus, although I didn't then know why. I didn't think of them as the key to a lock, because I didn't then see that there's a lock which severely restricts, or locks up, the freedom and creativity of most men and women.

Some time after I first wrote about the key virtues, a law partner of mine put on my desk a copy of Robert Wright's *The Moral Animal,* a description of the current state of the science of evolutionary psychology. I read it, and several other related books on anthropology and evolution, with great interest. Gradually, I began to see that evolutionary psychology, together with René Girard's cultural anthropology, which I'll discuss in Chapter 3, describes a lock limiting human freedom, and that the five commandments of Jesus are the key to this lock, the means of releasing the human freedom so restricted. The description of the lock begins with the study of certain behavioral inclinations which are common to all human beings because they are genetically based.

John Locke argued, in his *Essay Concerning Human Understanding,* that the human mind begins life as a white paper, void of all characters, without any ideas, a *tabula rasa.* If this applies to built-in predispositions or inclinations to act in certain ways, and not in others, it isn't true. There has developed over the last couple of generations the science of Darwinian anthropology, or evolutionary psychology, the study of genetically based human behavior patterns. Of particular interest to evolutionary psychologists has been the examination of a set of human behavior patterns which both (a) enhanced the fitness for survival and reproduction of hominids (and their evolutionary predecessors) which possessed such behavior patterns, and thus were embedded in the human genome by natural selection, and (b) seriously interfere with human efforts to live a life of freedom and moral decency in civilized societies.

Scholars have identified four such patterns. They are violence against other humans, acquisitiveness and greed, kinship loyalty combined with fear and hatred of strangers, and dominant-submissive patterns of conduct. Some evolutionary psychologists have concentrated their studies on the genetically based inclination toward violence, including rape, murder, war, and genocide. Others have given more attention to kinship selection or to dominant-submissive behaviors. I'll treat all four behaviors as of equal importance for my purposes.

Evolutionary psychologists have gone to considerable effort to establish, against the cultural behaviorists, that these behaviors aren't simply cultural behaviors but are actually found in our genes. This distinction is important. Genetically based behaviors are to be found in all humans with little variation. (Such variations in these behaviors as are found are due to cultural modification.) Genetically based anti-social behaviors are uniform throughout all humanity through all ages, because they pass from generation to generation by procreation, and they remained unchanged unless modified by natural selection. Culturally based behaviors can and do overlay these genetically based behaviors, and can work with them or against them, as we choose. Culturally based behaviors can pass from one generation to another only by teaching and example; they can't pass by procreation. So in each generation we have some responsibility for, and some control over, the transmission of our culturally based behaviors, but none over the transmission of our genetically based behaviors.

We can therefore make progress from generation to generation against amoral or immoral culturally based behaviors if we can make lasting improvements in the culture. But we can't make progress from generation to generation by changing or improving our genetically based behaviors. We can't change the human genome. No matter how we change and improve society, every human being will always have to work and struggle to control and overcome our genetically based behaviors. The only thing we can do is create and build cultural patterns of behavior which help individuals resist and overcome anti-social genetically based behaviors.

Because of this distinction, we need to be able to distinguish genetically based behaviors from culturally based behaviors. So we need to follow rather closely how the genetic basis for the behaviors identified as genetic by the evolutionary psychologists has been established.

There are two indicators that a specific behavior is genetic. First, behavioral characteristics can find their way into our genes if and only if those behaviors consistently conferred a reproductive advantage on those individuals (human or pre-human) which possessed them, and thus could have been, and probably were, naturally selected. Second, if we see similar patterns of behavior in the great apes and in other animals, that evidence confirms the conclusion that those behavior patterns evolved by natural selection and are in the human genome, because human cultural development can't account for their presence in animals.

Let's examine the behaviors listed above, one by one, for their possession of a reproductive advantage and for their presence in animals.

Violence. Why are men so violent? There's an obvious answer. A fundamental difference between men and women, and between males and females of almost every mammal species, is the very large difference in time commitment required for a given reproductive opportunity. The male impregnates the egg of the female, and he's done. The female has just begun. She must bear the fertilized egg, then the embryo, then the fetus, to birth, and, in mammals, nurse the newborn until it is weaned. A male is most successful in getting his genes to the next generation if he mates with as many females as possible, as often as possible. From the male point of view, the lengthy time commitment required of the female for reproduction, during which she's unavailable for new reproductive activity, very severely limits the available reproductive opportunities for males. So males compete with each other for reproductive opportunity. (It's good we have scientists to tell us about this.)

In many species, including all primates, this is a violent competition. Male gorillas regularly fight to the death to win and then preserve exclusive mating opportunities with a group of females. The victor in these fights gets his genes to the next generation; the vanquished does not. The genes of the bigger, stronger, quicker, more aggressive, and more violent males increase in frequency in the population with each generation. Natural selection thus selects for violence and aggressive behavior, particularly (but not exclusively) in males. This is why males have more testosterone and why men are generally bigger and stronger than women, as male gorillas are bigger and stronger than female gorillas.

Acquisitiveness. Isn't avarice a cultural thing? We're manipulated by advertising to buy things, and so forth? Not exactly. Acquisitiveness goes back to our hominid ancestors, and it too arises from the difference between males and females. Females generally don't need to compete with each other to get males willing to reproduce; there's usually an oversupply of ready males. Females can generally select among available males. In many animal species, females select for fitness, strength, aggression, and dominance. Natural selection will reward females who select for these qualities by making it more likely that their offspring, particularly their male offspring, will have these traits and will themselves survive and successfully reproduce. But significantly, among the higher primates and humans, females also select for signs of male parental investment: that is, indications that the male will still be around during the periods of gestation and infancy to provide protection to mother and offspring.

In the hominid period from as long as two million years ago, the size of the brain in the direct ancestors of humans increased threefold. There was no similar increase in the size of the birth canal during that period; successful live births were those that occurred ever earlier in the gestation period. The result of this evolution is that human newborns are far more helpless than newborns of other species. It became more and more important to the hominid female to have a male around to provide not only protection but food and shelter during this prolonged infancy period. Successful females thus selected not only for strength and fitness, but also for male parental investment and wealth, even if the wealth was nothing more than weapons for hunting and control of a place of shelter. Thus males which acquired possessions or control of territory and showed their ability to get and keep them were more frequently selected by females. Possession of goods, the desire for territory, and the willingness and ability to use violence if necessary to obtain them, was thus favored by natural selection.

Kinship Altruism. Charles Darwin had a difficult problem. He delayed the publication of *The Origin of Species* for many years while he tried to solve it. In some species of ants, sterile ants will instinctively fight to the death to defend the ant colony. In some species, bees, including sterile bees, will instinctively sting any animal threatening the hive, even though they die when they sting. Darwin's problem was to determine how an instinct which causes death, or an instinct found in sterile creatures, gets transmitted by natural selection. He found two closely-related and overlapping answers:

First, natural selection favors altruism within a family or kinship group. If an ant or a bee has the genetic trait of willingness to fight to the death for the colony, or to die without reproducing for the hive, that genetic trait will be found in the surviving and reproducing members of the colony or hive as well, because as kin they share the same genes. The labor or defense supplied by the non-reproducing members protects the colony or hive and thus gives a reproductive advantage to the reproducing kin of the non-reproducing members. Thus self-sacrificing genetic behavior survives and can be naturally selected.

It's similar with humans and other higher animals. Any behavioral attribute of a parent which enhances the survival and fitness of offspring will be favored by natural selection, because such activity helps the transmission of the parents' genes to the generation of grandchildren. A parent, wishing all of its offspring to survive and reproduce, will train or teach the offspring to share, not to fight with each other, and to support and care for one another. These activities will be favored by natural selection. Affection, loyalty, and altruism among siblings and cousins enhance the probability of survival and reproduction for all the members of the kinship group.

Second, cooperative activity within a group will sometimes itself enhance the probability of survival and reproduction of members of the group, whether there's a blood relationship among its members or not. A group of chimpanzees or of hominids can hunt or make war more effectively as a cooperative group than as lone individuals, and that's the way they hunted and fought. It's likely that this kind of cooperative behavior originated with kinship cooperation, gradually extending to more distant kin. To the extent that cooperation among members of a group enhances the survival of its members, it'll be selected by natural selection.

Kinship altruism and cooperative group altruism are both a long way from altruism toward all the individuals who are members of one's species. In many important ways, kinship altruism and group altruism are diametrically opposed to universal altruism. The kinship group naturally identifies itself in contrast with, and in opposition to, those who aren't kin. The cooperative group frequently achieves its unity in the bonding activity of war and pillage against those outside the group. The eminent biologist Ernst Mayr states this conclusion as follows:

> The same kinds of altruism that are extended to other members of a social group are rarely offered to outsiders. Different social groups usually compete with each other and not infrequently fight each other. There is little doubt that hominid history is a history of genocide. Indeed, the same can apparently be said about chimpanzees. How then could . . . . altruism toward outsiders have become established in the human species? Could natural selection be invoked? This has often been tried, but not very successfully. It is difficult to construct a scenario in which benevolent behavior toward competitors and enemies could be rewarded by natural selection. It is interesting in this connection to read the Old Testament and see how consistently a difference is made between behavior toward one's own group and behavior to any outsiders. This is in total contrast to the ethics promoted in the New Testament. Jesus's parable of the altruism of the Good Samaritan was a striking departure from custom. *Altruism toward strangers is a behavior not supported by natural selection.*

Some students of ethical behavior have argued that natural selection supports a kind of "reciprocal altruism," by which we respond with good deeds to the stranger who does good to us and respond with hostility and punishment to the stranger who offers non-cooperation. This strategy, the "tit-for-tat" strategy studied in Robert Axelrod's *The Evolution of Cooperation*, is argued to be close enough to universal altruism to work. But it doesn't.

Strategic reciprocal altruism is too intellectual and too calculated to serve as a moral guide to ordinary humans. Controlled and limited retaliation for another's fault or failure is after all not a new idea; it's the *lex talionis*. The command of the Lord (in Exodus 21:24-25 and in

Leviticus 24:20) that retaliation for wrongdoing be "eye for eye, tooth for tooth, hand for hand, foot for foot, burn for burn, wound for wound, stripe for stripe" (this is the *lex talionis*) was meant to limit retaliation, not encourage it. But if history teaches us anything, it teaches us that retaliation almost inevitably exceeds the original injury and provokes a reciprocal and escalated response in return. Measured and strategically calibrated retaliation requires dispassionate control and restraint. "Tit-for-tat" ethics can't be relied upon to guide and control normal human emotional reactions and passions in a threatening or violent situation. Even the most cursory reflection upon the consequences of kinship behavior in the contemporary world – the intransigent mutual hostility of Shiites and Sunnis, Palestinians and Israelis, Serbs and Kosevars, Hutus and Tutsi, and so forth – shows that reciprocal altruism, however carefully calibrated, falls far short of universal altruism.

Dominant-Submissive and Hierarchical Behaviors. Within many groups of animals, there have evolved behaviors in which individuals test their strength against others within the kinship or tribal group in contests which establish social ranking but stop short of mortal injury or death. Chimpanzee communities are closed groups within which a distinct social ranking system exists. Ranking within the community is established and maintained by fighting and by intimidation behavior which rarely results in serious injury to the combatants. Natural selection favors such behaviors because they enhance survival and provide stability to the closed group, while in contrast natural selection would not favor intra-group fighting to the death.

A familiar example of hierarchical behavior in animals is found in the term "pecking order," which describes the behavior of hens. If we put a group of hens together, there will initially be a period of instability, dispute, and combat. After a time, the hens settle down into a linear hierarchy. Hen A pecks Hen B, Hen B pecks Hen C, and so on. Each hen dominates those lower than her in the hierarchy and submits to the hens above her. Humans do the same thing in a much more complicated way. Dominance-submission hierarchies are found in many mammals and in all primates, including humans.

Summary. Natural selection, which permitted hominids to evolve from the great apes, and humans from the hominids, gave the earliest humans a genetic system with some built-in genetic behavior patterns.

The first humans, the ancestors of all of us, were violent. Their males were highly-evolved and successful fighters, hunters, and killers. They desired possessions and secure territory, and they were willing and able to fight other kinship or tribal groups to the death to acquire and hold them. They were loyal to and cooperative with kin, and with fellow members of their tribe or clan, and suspicious and fearful of, and hostile to, all others. Their tribes or clans were dominant-submissive hierarchical organizations, with chiefs, priests, workers, subjugated women, and slaves. So much for the Garden of Eden, and the life of the first humans in Paradise!

It's a sobering thought to realize that these behavior patterns, which were bred into the genes of the earliest humans by natural selection, are still in the genetic makeup of every human now alive. Natural selection is very slow, and ten thousand generations (roughly the time span since the emergence of Homo Sapiens) is a very short time on the clock of evolution. (Ten thousand generations for the average bacterium, reproducing every twenty minutes, take less than five months; that's why bacteria evolve so rapidly.) The human genome has not changed significantly since the dawn of humanity.

Even over a much longer period of time, there's very little chance that the human genome will change so as to reduce or eliminate these behavioral tendencies. Natural selection, having selected a genetic adaptation which enhances fitness to survive and reproduce in a particular environment, doesn't as a rule eliminate that adaptation when it's no longer needed or desirable. We all still have appendixes, even though they perform no useful function. If humans had been intelligently designed from scratch to walk on two legs, instead of being incrementally adapted from four-legged ancestors, people wouldn't so frequently suffer from back trouble. As back trouble doesn't ordinarily affect our fitness to survive and reproduce, it hasn't been subject to alleviation or elimination by natural selection. There's no reason to think that avoidance of violence, of hunger for possessions, of kinship loyalty, or of dominant-submissive behavior would increase any individual's chances of survival or reproductive opportunity in a way which would cause these genetic behaviors to be selected against. Natural selection doesn't have the betterment of the species as a goal. Even if these behaviors are in many ways obsolete or even harmful, we have retained and will retain them in our genetic material for the future, as we'll still have appendixes and bad backs.

Let's look again at the five commandments of Jesus. What do they have to say about the naturally selected human behaviors described above? Let's take each of the genetically based behaviors, the teachings of Jesus about it, and my paraphrase of each commandment, one by one:

Violence. "Do not resist an evildoer. If anyone strikes you on the right cheek, turn the other also" (Mt 5:39). "Love your enemies, do good to those who hate you" (Lk 6:27; Mt 5:44). DO NOT DO VIOLENCE TO ANY PERSON, EVEN IN RESPONSE TO VIOLENCE.

Acquisitiveness. "Do not store up for yourselves treasures on earth, where moth and rust consume and where thieves break in and steal; but store up for yourselves treasures in heaven" (Mt 6:19-20; Lk 12:33). DETACH YOURSELF FROM POSSESSIONS.

Kinship Altruism. "Do not judge, so that you may not be judged. . . Why do you see the mote in your neighbor's eye, but do not see the beam in your own eye?" (Mt 7:1,3; Lk 6:37, 41). "Forgive, and you will be forgiven" (Lk 6:37; Mt 6:14). DO NOT JUDGE, BLAME, CONDEMN, OR EXCLUDE ANY PERSON FROM YOUR FELLOWSHIP AND LOVE. FORGIVE ALL WHO HAVE OFFENDED YOU.

Dominant-Submissive Behavior. "The greatest among you will be your servant. All who exalt themselves will be humbled, and all who humble themselves will be exalted" (Mt 23:11-12; Lk 14:11). ACT AS A HUMBLE SERVANT TOWARD ALL OTHERS.

This is a remarkable result. Jesus could have preached about any number of ethical problems, and could have advocated any number of virtuous habits, most of which would have had nothing to do with naturally selected behaviors. But instead we find that *all* of his principal ethical teachings are directed at naturally selected behaviors. Jesus could have directed his attention to a few of these behaviors. Instead he spoke to *all* the principal naturally selected behaviors identified above and studied by contemporary evolutionary psychologists. He could have proposed compromises with these behaviors, of the sort we are familiar with in the Christian tradition – just war theory; the importance of patriotism and defending the nation against its "ene-mies"; family values, such as patriarchy; and the less said about acquisitiveness, the happier the congregation will be – but he didn't.

He advocated the most radical opposition to these behaviors, radical in the sense of digging them out by the roots. Indeed, there has been a long-lasting dispute in the Christian tradition about whether these teachings are simply very difficult, or whether they're impossible to a Christian living in the world (rather than in a monastery or convent) and can't be applied in the public sphere at all. We'll consider these questions in Chapters 7 and 8 below.

Jesus didn't know the Darwinian theory of evolution. He didn't know of Mendel's discovery of genetics or of Watson's and Crick's discovery of the double helix of DNA. He didn't know the work of contemporary evolutionary psychologists. How did he identify the naturally selected and genetically based behaviors of humanity, and how and why did he select them as the objects of his principal ethical teachings? However he did it, the five commandments of Jesus constitute a profound anthropological observation, or reflection, or (perhaps) revelation. Jesus clearly thought, and in his five commandments said, that the fundamental problem of humanity is the set of naturally selected behaviors against which his five commandments are directed.

Some of you may observe that Jesus doesn't expressly identify the behaviors against which his five commandments are directed. But consider: If a doctor prescribes a good night's sleep, there may be doubt about his diagnosis. If he prescribes aspirin, he has probably diagnosed a headache, or perhaps bodily pain. But if he prescribes a complex regimen of retroviral drugs, there's little doubt what his diagnosis is. The principal ethical teachings of Jesus, his five commandments, are a complex and precisely-tailored prescription for the cure of our genetically based ailments, and thus a precise diagnosis of those ailments.

Observe that what's new and different in the ethical teachings of Jesus isn't the golden rule, or the "great commandment" to love one's neighbor as oneself, or the command to love one another. All these had been discovered and taught in the great spiritual discoveries of the Axial Age (900 B.C.–200 B.C.). What's new and different in the teachings of Jesus is the description of the precise behaviors, the genetically based behaviors, to be resisted and overcome, and the prescription of very specific attitudes and practices directed at such behaviors and intended to replace them with new and opposing attitudes and practices.

* * * * *

There's a second set of behaviors, proper to humans, which is also genetically based, although it's not found in other animals, but is a consequence of the evolution of the reflective and self-conscious human mind. Human freedom, or conscious self-direction, is made possible by a severe attenuation of our animal instincts. We aren't driven by instinct, but we are driven, to a large extent, by our desires. Two consequences of this development make human life difficult:

First, in the normal course of human development, we first learn and experience desires and only later, and with difficulty, learn to control and order our desires. Most of us learn from our mistakes. Mistakes and occasional failures of control of our desires are virtually inevitable for all of us. Habitual failures of control are not infrequent.

Reflect for a moment on your own childhood. Remember how hard it was to learn the control each of us needs to function in the family and in society and how inevitable are mistakes and failures of control. Consider, for example, the desire and need for food. The baby wants to be fed when he or she is hungry. In the course of a normal childhood, the child is gradually taught to control this desire and to eat moderate quantities at regular times. The desire for more always reasserts itself, and controlling and ordering this desire is often difficult, even for us as adults. Consider learning to tell the truth. As most of us will remember, a child usually learns to tell the truth only after he or she has been caught telling a lie to his or her parents and has been punished for it.

Second, with many objects of desire, we learn what we desire from others. That is, in the absence of specific instinctual desires, our desire is often imitative, or mimetic. Consider two little boys in a room full of toys. One little boy chooses a toy. The other little boy usually then desires that chosen toy rather than any of the other toys in the room, precisely because it has been shown to him as desirable. So he grabs for that toy, and the two little boys start fighting.

Imitative or mimetic desire naturally produces the conflict of the double bind. The father says to his son, "Your mother is the most wonderful woman in the world. You must *love* her the way I do. No, on second thought, you must *never* love her the *way* I do." The lover says to his best friend, "My love is the most beautiful lady and a paragon of virtue. Don't you agree?" Does the friend then lose his friend by disbelieving his statement? Or does he lose his friend by believing the statement and wooing the lady? Shakespeare explored exactly this conflict arising from mimetic rivalry in many of his comedies, such as *The Two Gentlemen of Verona* and *A Midsummer Night's Dream*. Similarly, in *Gone With the Wind,* Scarlett O'Hara desires Ashley Wilkes simply because Melanie Hamilton loves him. When she wins his hand, she quickly tires of him. Thus ordinary mimetic desire makes for great comedy and drama because it naturally leads to acts of disorder or conflict or both.

Did Jesus say anything about these genetically based behavior problems, those of desire, particularly imitative or mimetic desire, and the conflicts our desires naturally cause? It seems to me that Jesus addresses this problem in two ways:

First, the principal thrust of all the ethical teachings of Jesus is the control of desires. Four of the five commandments specifically call for a change in our minds, in our habits of looking at the world: do not judge, forgive, be a humble servant, and become detached from possessions. Only the commandment not to do violence describes and prohibits an external act, and that commandment can't be obeyed without serious mental preparation and internal control. In contrast, five of the second tablet commandments of Moses direct or prohibit particular external acts, and only the commandment against coveting expressly calls for a change of mind. The teaching of Jesus that "everyone who looks at a woman with lust has already committed adultery with her in his heart" (Mt 5:28) is another example of the way Jesus has shifted the focus of ethical conduct from the external act to the internal disposition.

Second, Jesus dealt with imitative or mimetic desire by holding himself out as the sole mimetic mentor, that is, as the unique leader whose words should be followed and whose example should be imitated by his disciples. Jesus said,

> A disciple is not above the teacher, nor a servant above the master; it is enough for the disciple to be like the teacher, and the servant like the master. (Mt 10:24-25; Lk 6:40; Jn 13:16)

> But you are not to be called rabbi, for you have one teacher, and you are all students. And call no one your father on earth, for you have one Father – the one in heaven. Nor are

you to be called teachers, for you have one teacher, the Messiah. (Mt 23:8-10)

I am the light of the world. Whoever follows me will never walk in darkness but will have the light of life. (Jn 8:12)

I am the way, and the truth, and the life. No one comes to the Father except through me. (Jn 14:6)

Jesus never left it in doubt that he was the one master, the one instructor, the one exemplar, and the one mediator of God's will for men and women. We should learn what to desire from watching him and listening to him.

We started this chapter looking for the lock which would match the key of the five commandments. The naturally selected and genetically based behaviors of humans are clearly the lock which this key can open. But this gets us only to prehistoric and primitive humans. Before returning to the history of Jesus, we need to see how the genetically based anti-social behaviors we have identified were and are incorporated into our human social, cultural, and political institutions. The first step is to explore the history of ancient civilizations, to see the origin and development of that peculiar institution, the human sacrifice, and to see how ancient civilizations dealt with and built upon humanity's genetic behavioral heritage.

Meanwhile, we're adding complexities to the picture we're building of Jesus of Nazareth. We have a woodworker from Nazareth, of humble origins and provincial background, who embarked upon a short career as an itinerant preacher and healer. He believed, and those around him believed, that he could heal the sick, the blind, the deaf, and the lame, and raise the dead to life. He spoke with authority, directly and in brilliant imaginative figures. His principal ethical teachings showed a command of cultural anthropology and evolutionary psychology. And he had an exalted sense of his own position in relation to the dealings of men and women with each other and with God. All of this is history. We haven't yet come to theology or religion.

Notes and Sources for Further Reading

John Locke, *An Essay Concerning Human Understanding,* in Burtt, Edwin A., ed., *The English Philosophers from Bacon to Mill* (Modern Library, 1939), p. 248 (Book II, Ch. 1, para 2).

Robert Wright's book, *The Moral Animal* (Vintage Books, 1994), is a particularly fine presentation of the topic of evolutionary psychology.

Michael P. Ghiglieri, in his book *The Dark Side of Man* (Perseus Books, 1999), concentrates on male violence as a genetic trait.

Irenaus Eibl-Eibesfeldt's book, *The Biology of Peace and War* (Viking Press, 1979), deals with violence and warfare in the anthropology of hominids and of primitive humans.

Ernst Meyr's book, *What Evolution Is* (Basic Books, 2001), is an excellent introduction to the theory of evolution and the principles of natural selection. Meyr was Professor Emeritus in the Museum of Comparative Zoology at Harvard University, and was called (before his recent death) the world's greatest living evolutionary biologist. He published his first scientific paper in 1923, and his last in 2003! The quotation (with emphasis added) is from pp. 258-59.

Robert Axelrod, *The Evolution of Cooperation* (Basic Books, 1984).

Malcolm Potts and Thomas Hayden, in their book *Sex and War* (Benbella Books, 2008), explore in great detail the same genetically based anti-social behaviors of humans as those identified here, and show how they remain at the roots of contemporary society's most difficult problems.

For an excellent and thorough treatment of the Axial Age, see Karen Armstrong's *The Great Transformation* (Alfred A. Knopf, 2006).

René Girard's book, *A Theater of Envy* (Oxford University Press, 1991), is a brilliant study of mimetic desire in the plays of Shakespeare; his book, *Deceit, Desire and the Novel* (Johns Hopkins Press, 1966), is an equally brilliant study of mimetic desire in the novels of Cervantes, Stendhal, Proust, and Dostoevsky.

The Genetically Based Behaviors and the Five Commandments of Jesus:

Violence.	"Do not resist an evildoer. If anyone strikes you on the right cheek, turn the other also." (Mt 5:39) "Love your enemies, do good to those who hate you." (Lk 6:27; Mt 5:44)	DO NOT DO VIOLENCE TO ANY PERSON, EVEN IN RESPONSE TO VIOLENCE.
Acquisitiveness.	"Do not store up for yourselves treasures on earth, where moth and rust consume and where thieves break in and steal; but store up for yourselves treasures in heaven." (Mt 6:19-20; Lk 12:33)	DETACH YOURSELF FROM POSSESSIONS.
Kinship Altruism.	"Do not judge, so that you may not be judged. … Why do you see the mote in your neighbor's eye, but do not see the beam in your own eye?" (Mt 7:1,3; Lk 6:37, 41) "Love your enemies, do good to those who hate you." (Lk 6:27) "Forgive, and you will be forgiven." (Lk 6:37; Mt 6:14-15)	DO NOT JUDGE, BLAME, CONDEMN OR EXCLUDE ANY PERSON FROM YOUR FELLOWSHIP AND LOVE. FORGIVE ALL WHO HAVE OFFENDED YOU.
Dominant-Submissive Behavior.	"The greatest among you will be your servant. All who exalt themselves will be humbled, and all who humble themselves will be exalted." (Mt 23:11-12; Lk 14:11)	ACT AS A HUMBLE SERVANT TOWARD ALL OTHERS.

III

THE WORLD OF SACRIFICE

"He [the devil] was a murderer from the beginning." (Jn 8:44)

To SEE HOW HUMAN CIVILIZATIONS dealt with the genetically based anti-social behaviors of human beings, we need first to look at one of the oldest of human cultural institutions, the practice of human sacrifice. Human sacrifice was universal and central in ancient and primitive religious practices. How and why did it arise and root itself so deeply? It's not in our genetic inheritance. It's hard to think of anything less likely to be favored by natural selection than human sacrifice. It's a cultural institution.

What does human sacrifice have to do with the genetically based behaviors? Just this: as the oldest cultural institution of humanity, it was the first human institution to channel, and thus control, these behaviors. It didn't resist or oppose these behaviors, but incorporated them into its rituals and myths, and it was the first of a long line of human institutions to internalize and regulate these behaviors. So we begin with human sacrifice. I preface this discussion with two observations:

First, let's be clear on the terminology. By "sacrifice" I mean a ritual ceremony in which a community, in the firm belief that it will be pleasing to their god, selects a representative victim, a scapegoat, and kills the victim. Think of the Aztecs: the priests, the virginal victims, the processions, the glistening knives, the flowing blood. The Israelites believed in and practiced sacrifice in this way, although they substituted a bull or a goat for the human victim. See Leviticus 16.

The word "sacrifice" is sometimes used to describe something entirely different, which is better called "self-sacrifice." This is the altruistic act of a person who is willing to put himself or herself in harm's way to save the life of another, or to remain steadfast to his or her own principles. As familiar examples of the former, think of the soldier in the foxhole who falls on the hand grenade to save the lives of his buddies, or the firefighters who ran up the stairs of the burning World Trade Center towers just before the buildings collapsed. As examples of the latter, think of the Christian martyrs who refused to worship idols, or of John McCain in the North Vietnam prison when he refused to sign a "confession" of his "crimes." Self-sacrifice isn't what I'm talking about.

Second, in modern times, it's very difficult for us to have any real imaginative understanding of ritual religious sacrifice. We recoil at the ritual sacrifices of the Aztecs. It's almost impossible for us to imagine that the Aztec priests, or many of them at any rate, actually thought they were doing what was good and necessary for their people as they officiated at their ceremonies and killed their victims. But they did. It's almost impossible for us to understand that, as a matter of course, priests and people really believed that the sacrificial victim was guilty of the disorder and social evil the ritual sacrifice was intended to avert. But they did. So we must make a considerable imaginative effort to understand the ancient sacrifice, and how it really worked.

We begin with a "Which came first, the chicken or the egg?" question. If we start with the god or gods which require the sacrifice, and then proceed to the sacrifice itself, it's quite difficult to imagine how the practice of sacrifice could have begun. We can imagine a primitive tribe in some sort of distress, praying to whatever gods they believe in to save them. But when we ourselves are in distress, the last thing in the world we'd think to do is to select one of our neighbors, or, more likely, go down to the bus station and select a stranger in town, and kill him or her in a formal ritual. Yet this is what ancient humans did all over the world.

It's not an answer to say that they believed that the gods desired or demanded sacrifice. That just leaves us with an even more difficult question: how in the world did ancient humans ever invent a belief in gods who desired human sacrifice? In my view, we can work out an explanation of sacrifice only if we start with a collective murder at a time of distress, and then see how the murder, and the resulting guilt and shame, caused the people to invent the gods which demanded sacrifices.

Equally perplexing is the question, how does sacrifice work? Ancient humans would not have so universally and for so long made human sacrifice the center of their religious rituals and myths, and made religious rituals and myths the center of their cultures, unless sacrifice really worked to change, to strengthen, and to bind the people in some meaningful way. But it's difficult to see how this could be so.

The French scholar René Girard has advanced a hypothesis which explains the mechanism of human sacrifice and its centrality in ancient and primitive civilizations. His explanation of sacrifice is persuasive and illuminating. I know of no other theory which so well accounts for the origin of sacrifice. The clearest way to explain Girard's theory is to set forth the scenario in which sacrifice originates:

Let's imagine a typical tribe of the very earliest humans prior to any laws, rules, or taboos. As must have frequently happened, two young males start a fight over a woman or over a prize of some sort which both desire. The fighting escalates, and more young males, friends or relatives of one or the other, become involved; one combatant is killed, and vengeance is required; a blood feud starts. Each act of violence produces a responding act of reciprocal violence, and soon the whole community is involved. The survival of the community is threatened, because there's no way to stop the violence, and if it continues, all the males will kill each other.

But this time, in this tribe, the creative imagination of the elders produces a solution. The growing hatred, violence, and reciprocal vengeance within the community can't be stopped, but it can be channeled, from the hatred of all-against-all to the hatred of all-against-one, preferably an outsider, a "scapegoat," a victim without a family to take vengeance for his or her death. The elders find a potential victim – a stranger, a virgin, a widow without issue, or a cripple – and identify him or her as the source of the tribe's troubles. Eager to hear this, the tribe unites against the chosen one, focusing their anger and violence on him or her, and they kill the victim. The community is now united in guilt and horror at its collective murder, and yet relieved that no one will seek vengeance for the death of the sacrificial victim. The sacrifice of the victim thus ends the cycle of reciprocal and escalating violence within the tribe. The community is temporarily at peace.

The violence within the tribe will break out again. But when it does, the elders of the tribe know what to do. Another victim will be selected, another human sacrifice will be performed, and this time it'll be performed in ritual fashion, with elaborate routines and rubrics, so that it'll achieve the same result. This is the origin of sacrifice.

The people of the tribe, seeking to avoid guilt for their collective murder of an innocent victim, develop a simple and very human excuse for their crime. They transfer to the victim both the blame for the initial violence and disorder and the credit for its surcease. This critically important transfer exonerates the people of the tribe. It also makes the victim a sacred being, a hero, a savior, and a god, because the victim has by his or her death brought peace to the tribe.

The elders who officiated at the ritual sacrifice of the sacred victim have now become priests, intermediating between the people and the sacred victim, and in the name of the sacred victim they proclaim the first prohibitions and taboos. Since a frequent cause of the outbreak of male aggression and violence which started the whole problem would naturally be fighting over women, the first prohibitions were usually those against murder and incest. The taboo against murder is self-explanatory. The taboo against incest has nothing to do with interbreeding or genetics. It was intended to prohibit sex within the immediate family, simply to prevent males from fighting over the women in the family and killing their own fathers, brothers, or sons.

The community has now transferred to the sacred victim, and to the sacred "god" which the victim now represents, the blame and the credit for the sacrifice which has united the community and has saved it from its own self-destructive violence. The victim is now understood to be the one who originated the sacrifice. The community now describes its "god" as a god who requires and demands sacrifice.

The practice of human sacrifice, which is now a religious act, thus involves two real psychological transferences: first, responsibility for the violence and for the sacrificial murder is transferred from the community to the victim; and second, responsibility for requiring the sacrificial murder is transferred from the community to the god the victim has become. This description of the sacrifice, and of these transferences, is then embodied in the ritual of the tribe and preserved in the community's founding myth. The victim of the first sacrifice is transmuted into the god itself, a god who by his or her death creates the community and who requires ritual sacrifice. Founding myths of this sort usually disguise the underlying murder, but it's always there.

Many examples of such founding myths could be given. One short example is a tale of the Montagnais Indians of eastern Quebec, the Legend of the North Star:

People of another (earlier) world were living in a village. They knew a new world was going to be formed. One day a number of them started to quarrel. One of the number was North Star. The others fell on him, meaning to kill him, but he fled and soared into the sky. All started after, but when they saw they could not get him: "Well," they said, "let him be! He is North Star. He will be of use to the people of the world that is to come, as a guide by night to their travels."

In this brief tale we see all the elements of the primeval human sacrifice. There was violence among a number of the villagers. The violence is focused on one scapegoat, North Star. He is certainly killed, but the story disguises the murder. He was probably driven off a cliff (he "soared into the sky"), which is a common form of sacrificial execution. It's an ancient way of collective murder, like stoning, in which all participate and no one singly inflicts the death blow. The victim is now a sacred being, and from this time a new world is formed, the "world that is to come."

It's critical to the efficacy of the sacrifice that the community really transfers its guilt and blame for the murder to the victim. This is a lie, an act of communal self-deception. It's the primal lie. But it was not seen as such. This was a communal murder, and the murderers felt no guilt. It's hard for modern people to see how complete the psychological transference of guilt to the victim was. But think about the white men who took part in the lynching of African-Americans in the American South and Midwest in the late nineteenth and early twentieth centuries. Most of them really believed that they were doing the right thing, and that all the blame and all the guilt were properly placed on the lynched victim.

What comes out of this primal sacrifice and its regularly repeated ritual reenactment? What had previously been a tribe, with only the cohesion of kinship, now has rules of conduct and universal ethical prohibitions against murder, incest, stealing, and so forth. It now has rituals with painstakingly detailed rubrics, which are important because the primal sacrifice must be exactly reproduced to have its effect. It now has a class of priests who celebrate the ritual sacrifice and who observe specified rules of diet, dress, and cleanness to set themselves apart and maintain their ritual purity. It now has something other than blood to bind and unite the community and set it apart from, and make it superior to, those of their neighbors: a religion. (The root of the word "religion" is the Latin *religare*, which means "to bind.") In short, there's now a community with a complex human culture, which I call the "culture of sacrifice."

See what has happened to the genetically based anti-social behaviors. Violence at its worst, in the form of a collective murder of an innocent victim, has been placed at the center of the primitive religion. The community as a kinship group judges the victim to be an outcast, worthy of condemnation and death. The community transfers blame for the murder to the victim, which means both that it can't forgive the victim for his or her faults, real or imagined, and that it can't seek forgiveness for its own crime, because it has denied that a crime took place. The community has created a dominant class, the priests, to which all others submit. If, as is probably the case, men rather than women actually killed the sacrificial victim, this would raise the ritual status of men in the community and contribute to the subjugation of its women.

The culture of sacrifice "worked" for the earliest humans because it provided what was most necessary for humanity to begin human culture: a mechanism which brought the otherwise anti-social genetically based behavior patterns of humans under social control. The primary purpose and effect of the sacrifice itself was to arrest, control, and sublimate the violence of the members of the tribe, particularly the young males. The rituals, observances, and taboos of the primitive sacrificial religion provided a unifying bond within the community which superseded that of blood kinship, and involved all the members of the community in the ritual practices in an active way. This gave the community the ability to increase in size beyond that of a kinship group, a great advantage in the perpetual warfare among neighboring tribes. This would explain why the culture of sacrifice is virtually universal in ancient and primitive cultures. The tribes and clans which didn't invent or discover their own sacrificial religions would have been defeated in battle by the larger and stronger communities which had developed a culture of sacrifice.

The genius of the culture of sacrifice is that it didn't oppose the naturally-selected genetically based behaviors of humans. It channeled them. Violence against members of the community was forbidden, but the sacrifice itself was violent, and an outlet for violence, and warfare against strangers under the leadership of the hierarchy was encouraged and praised. Kinship altruism was broadened to include all those who worshiped and sacrificed together, but suspicion, fear, and hatred of strangers (so identified by the tribal leaders and priests), and warfare against them, was approved. Dominant-submissive behavior was not just permitted but required under the established hierarchy of priests and warriors, and so was concentration of wealth and power. Because the culture of sacrifice didn't resist the evolved genetic behavior patterns of humans, but instead internalized them and reinforced them with sacrificial rituals, myths, and rules of conduct, it has sunk deep roots into human psychology and human culture and has the strength of biologically evolved and culturally developed behaviors combined.

Evolutionary biologists have in the last forty years developed a concept called "evolutionary stability." A biological culture is evolutionarily stable if no single mutant can successfully invade the culture and change it. In his influential book, *The Evolution of Coopera-tion*, briefly discussed in the last chapter, David Axelrod applied the concept of evolutionary stability to game theory. A game strategy is evolutionarily stable if no single player following a different strategy can succeed in the game in a large group of players following the stable strategy. Axelrod argues that a life strategy, such as reciprocal altruism, can be analyzed the same way. For a game strategy, a moral strategy, or a biological culture to be successful over a long time period, it must be resistant to change. If it is so highly resistant to change that no single different strategy or mutation can change it significantly, it's said to have evolutionary stability.

The culture of sacrifice has this quality; it's evolutionarily stable. It's said of India that while India has been conquered many times, its ancient culture has always absorbed the conqueror's culture and has continued with little change. So the culture of sacrifice has always had the power to absorb and neutralize efforts to change it, and it has done so for thousands of years. We all see violence among men, warfare and persecution between ethnic or religious groups, extreme concentrations of wealth, and hierarchies of priests, mullahs, and business and military leaders in the news of the world every day. The culture of sacrifice has remained the world's most stable and dominant cultural institution.

The culture of sacrifice was already ancient when agriculture began and animals were domesticated some eight to ten thousand years ago. These developments permitted the concentration of larger populations in fixed settlements and the accumulation of wealth. Soon after, the earliest known cities were founded, and writing was invented. The most ancient urban civilizations we know of – Sumer, Babylon, and the cities of ancient Egypt, for example – date from that time. All these ancient cities were religious communities, united under a local god or gods. Their religions, expressed in their founding mythologies, were regulated by a priestly class and included elaborate ritual practices and regulations. They were military societies, led by a king-priest who was also a warrior leader of a warrior class. At the heart of their religions was the human sacrifice. These societies were (and of necessity had to be) communities of collective violence, engaged both in continual warfare against neighboring kingdoms, and in oppression and subjugation of their own lower classes, their women, and their slaves to the religious and military hierarchy.

The culture of sacrifice was humanity's first great invention. It was the indispensable invention, because it provided the mechanisms necessary to bring the genetically based behaviors of the earliest humans under social control. Without these mechanisms of control, the earliest humans could not have organized themselves in groups large enough to develop and preserve the later ancient inventions of human civilization. They would've killed each other first. Consider the situation of our nearest living relatives in the animal world, the gorillas and the chimpanzees. Gorillas live in groups no larger than one-male harems, averaging eight members. Chimpanzees live in kinship groups, generally with fewer than fifty members, and make war on neighboring groups. The human sacrifice made the difference, permitting growth of larger human communities.

Let's move forward to the time of Jesus and look at the Mediterranean world. Israel was then a small theocracy, with animal and plant sacrifices regularly performed in its most sacred place, the Temple in Jerusalem. In Greece, the religions of sacrifice were still practiced, but they were separated from the higher culture and the intellectual life of the nation. In Rome at the time of Caesar Augustus there were a great many cults and sects of religion and sacrifice, but the unity of the empire was based not on a common religion but on Roman military power, wealth, and effective civil administration. The culture of sacrifice had run its course. It had completed its great contribution to the progress of humanity.

But the lives of most men and women living within the culture of sacrifice, or in the ancient nations built on the foundation of sacrificial religions, were far from satisfactory. The internal discipline and cohesion of these nations were bought at a price. There was little room for individual freedom or creativity, except among the upper classes and the very wealthy. The virtues of humanity's childhood and adolescence had become the vices of humanity's maturity. The virtues of the most successful primitive tribes had been the controlled direction of violence away from other members of the tribe and onto outsiders, enforced ritual prohibitions and practices, and a rigorously hierarchical social system, all founded in a vigorous sacrificial religion. These virtues had served their limited purposes. Their time had passed. They became vices, locking societies into the suppression of individual freedom and initiative, regular suppression of the submissive, the downtrodden and those seen as "different" or "other," and endless war against other tribal, ethnic, or religious communities. The ultimate problem of humanity was and is this: the evolutionary stability of the culture of sacrifice and the cultures of the nations founded on its principles have become the principal obstacle to the continued development of human freedom and creativity.

There has been progress, of a sort. We don't have ritual human sacrifice in the modern world. We haven't had ritual human sacrifice in the Western world for two thousand years or more. The Hebrew Scriptures tell us that the Jews, while their religious practices always involved sacrifice, had from earliest times substituted animal sacrifice, or even plant sacrifice, for human sacrifice. In the ancient legends of Genesis, Cain and Abel sacrificed crops and lamb respectively (Gen 4:3-4). At least one point of the story of Abraham and Isaac is that God would accept the sacrifice of a ram in place of the sacrifice of Isaac, Abraham's only legitimate son and heir (Gen 22:1-14). The second book of Kings records two instances where kings of Judah, in the seventh and sixth centuries B.C., made blood sacrifices of their first-born sons (2 Kings 16:3-4; 21:6), but the chronicler records these as abominable acts. Ritual human sacrifice has effectively stopped wherever the Christian message has been preached.

But there is another form of human sacrifice, communal but not ritualized, which has survived. As we have seen, the critical element of the human sacrifice is the transfer of guilt and blame from the community which kills to the victim who is killed. Often in medieval and modern history we see instances in which a whole community kills an innocent victim or class of victims without any justification. The desire to avoid guilt and blame is very strong, and in many of those instances, where the community or its sympathetic chroniclers have written the story, they have recorded that the victims themselves were to blame. Three historic examples will illustrate:

1. At the time of the first great plague in Europe, about 1350, the Christians in many towns in France and Germany massacred many Jews. Their chroniclers recorded the prevailing rumors and stories, believed by them but unbelievable to us, in which the Christians blamed the Jews for the plague, claiming, among other things, that the Jews had drunk the blood of Christian children, had poisoned the rivers, and were to blame for their own deaths.

2. During the sixteenth and seventeenth centuries, in France, central Germany, Northern Italy, and several other European countries, a majority of Christians, Catholic and Protestant, in great distress from bad crops and from the religious warfare which then inflicted them, convinced themselves that there existed in their midst a dangerous conspiracy of witches, in league with the devil, with powers over nature. Every drought or crop failure was blamed on the witches. An inquisitorial legal process was set up to identify and eradicate this threat. By this process good Christians tried and executed over one hundred thousand alleged witches, nearly all women, and all innocent.

3. In the late nineteenth and early twentieth centuries, in the United States, white mobs lynched thousands of black men, few of whom were guilty of any crime. The lynchers firmly believed that they were doing the right thing, protecting white womanhood, and that the victims were to blame.

In these cases we can see all the elements of ancient human sacrifice. There was a general sense of social or cultural crisis; the victims were accused of fantastic and implausible crimes but were actually selected because of their membership in an outcast group; the victims were killed; and the mob transferred the guilt of the killing itself to the victim. Every element of sacrifice is present but the ritual, and even that isn't entirely absent. In *At the Hands of Persons Unknown: the Lynching of Black America*, Philip Dray observes that

The high degree of ritual seen in the Smith lynching and many others – the use of fire, the sacredness of the objects associated with the killing, the symbolic taking of trophies of the victim's remains, the sense of celebratory anticipation and then the lingering importance participants placed on such events – *all suggest an anthropological basis for viewing lynching as a form of tribal sacrifice.* Many observers commented on a lynching's ability to "clear the air," or described it as the kind of painful spasm a community "needed" in order to regain a feeling of normalcy, and many lynchings did occur in a climate of preexisting racial tensions – a fight between a black and a white, talk of insolence on the part of blacks, competition for jobs, an escalating exchange of insults, or the spread of damaging rumors.

Human sacrifice still exists, in events of "scapegoating" or lynching like these: witness the Holocaust, Cambodia, Rwanda. While the transfer of blame and guilt from the executioners to the victim still occurs, it was a lie from the beginning, and it's still a lie. It's this lie which makes it possible for violence, ethnic and religious hatred, dominant-submissive behaviors, and concentration of wealth in the midst of poverty to remain such fundamental parts of our culture. It's against this lie, and against these genetically based behaviors, that Jesus concentrated his ethical teachings.

Throughout the ages of the culture of sacrifice until the present, there has been considerable development of ethics, of rules and required practices for moral conduct. Have the ethical principles and practices so developed said anything about the evils embedded in the culture of sacrifice? Generally, no. The evils of the culture of sacrifice arise in large part from the incorporation of the genetically based anti-social behaviors of humans into the public institutions of humanity. But Christian ethical teaching has, throughout most of the history of the Christian churches, concerned itself almost exclusively with personal sin, not with social or communal sin.

Confessional manuals for the training of priests as confessors, based primarily on the ten commandments of Moses and the seven deadly sins (pride, covetousness, lust, anger, gluttony, envy, and sloth), were developed in or before the thirteenth century. As a general rule, practice of the ethics of the Sermon on the Mount was expected only in monastic communities. In the sixteenth century, Luther, Calvin, and other reformers attacked the confessional manuals and insisted on the centrality of the ten commandments of Moses for moral instruction. But the ten commandments, second table, are also primarily concerned with describing personal moral evil to be avoided: "Thou shalt not" kill, commit adultery, steal, lie, or covet another's wife or goods. Thus what the Jesuit scholar James Keenan calls "a long period of moral narcissism" began and continued, in which Christians, Catholic and Protestant, "became anxious not about the kingdom [of God] or the needs of the Church, but rather about the state of their individual souls."

With ethical teaching concentrated on avoiding the seven deadly sins, or the evils proscribed by the ten commandments, the Christian's attention has been focused on personal sin. This is strongly reinforced by the traditional Christian teaching that one serious sin, unrepented and unconfessed, is all it takes to damn your soul to hell for all eternity. The way to personal salvation is avoiding personal sin and confessing it if it isn't avoided. It's as if one sought guidance for living a happy and successful life by learning the criminal code, or good health by studying pathology.

In the course of history, as states developed criminal justice systems, the prohibitions against murder, robbery, burglary, assault and battery, and perjury were incorporated into the public law, leaving behind only the familial and sexual prohibitions for the churches. As the public law is obligatory on Christians and non-Christians alike, the absence of difference between the ethical lives of Christians and the ethical lives of non-Christians is as real as it is apparent. And when conservative Christian churches talk about ethics, they usually talk about family values and sexual prohibitions, even though Jesus said almost nothing about these areas of conduct.

Modern and contemporary commentators, including theologians and religious leaders, have recently redirected the study of Christian ethics from exclusive concentration on personal sin and its avoidance. They describe the moral evils embedded in societal structures and customs, and the evil consequences which ensue, as communal or social sin. Obvious examples of serious sin embedded in law or social custom are slavery, ethnic cleansing, the subjugation of women, and aggressive war, all of which flow from the genetically based anti-social behaviors internalized by human institutions.

Social sin doesn't respond to the traditional analysis of sin. For one thing, with social sin no one is guilty, or all are guilty. Moral responsibility for established social customs and institutions is hard to allocate, and allocating blame is harder. Yet, if you stop and think about it, far more people have been harmed by social sin than by personal sin. For another, personal sin is traditionally seen as a violation of law. Social sins, embodied in societal structures, are frequently embodied in society's laws, which the Christian churches have taught us are generally to be obeyed. Thus exclusive concentration on personal sin frequently supports rather than opposes social sin, and thus supports rather than opposes the culture of sacrifice.

Identification of social and institutional evils as true sins is a first step toward reaching the resolution to oppose them with moral force. This is what this chapter has been about: *the identification of the foundational social and institutional sins which are incorporated into the warp and woof of human social, cultural, and political institutions.* These evils are the result of the absorption of the genetically based anti-social behaviors into human institutions.

Did Jesus have in mind a "culture of sacrifice" to which he was opposed and against which he directed his teaching? I've described the culture of sacrifice in terms of (a) the behavior patterns of humans which evolved in our pre-human ancestors by natural selection, which presupposes the discoveries of Darwin and of the twentieth-century evolutionary psychologists, and (b) the cultural and religious patterns of prehistoric and ancient cultures throughout the world, which presupposes the anthropological and ethnological discoveries of the last two centuries. Could Jesus have seen the cultures of mankind in this way?

Actually, he seems to have done so; he (or, at least, the author of the Gospel of John) said so. What I've called the culture of sacrifice Jesus called the world, the flesh, or the devil. Jesus several times described himself as engaged in a struggle for the souls of mankind against a resistant, deceitful, and implacable adversary:

> To his brothers: "The world cannot hate you, but it hates me because I testify to it that its works are evil." (Jn 7:7)

To his disciples: "It is the spirit that gives life; the flesh is useless. The words that I have spoken to you are spirit and life." (Jn 6:63)

To the Jews: "You are from below, I am from above; you are of this world, I am not of this world." (Jn 8:23)

To the Jews: "You are from your father the devil, and you choose to do your father's desires. He was a murderer from the beginning and does not stand in the truth, because there is no truth in him. When he lies, he speaks according to his own nature, for he is a liar and the father of lies. But because I tell the truth, you do not believe me." (Jn 8:44-45)

To the crowd in Jerusalem: "Now is the judgment of this world; now the ruler of this world will be driven out. And I, when I am lifted up, will draw all people to myself." (Jn 12:31-32)

To his disciples: "If the world hates you, be aware that it hated me before it hated you. If you belonged to the world, the world would love you as its own. Because you do not belong to the world, but I have chosen you out of the world – therefore the world hates you." (Jn 15:18-19)

The "world" isn't the sinners; Jesus came to call and save the sinners. The "world," as Jesus used the term, is the culture of sacrifice, which hates Jesus because he gives testimony, in his teachings, that its works are evil. The culture of sacrifice, personified as the devil, is "a murderer from the beginning," because its central and primeval act is the ritual sacrifice of an innocent victim. The culture of sacrifice, personified as the devil, is "a liar, and the father of lies," because the critical psychological transference of guilt and blame from the community to the sacrificial victim is a lie, the fundamental and primal lie. Jesus opposed the culture of sacrifice with the truth, principally embodied in his five commandments: "The words that I have spoken to you are spirit and life"; "I testify to it that its works are evil"; and with his life, "When I am lifted up." Jesus declared victory over the culture of sacrifice: "Now is the judgment of the world; now the ruler of this world will be driven out." But he said the struggle would continue for his followers: "Therefore the world hates you."

Christians are, or should be, mutant invaders pursuing a different strategy within the evolutionarily stable civilization which still lives by the culture of sacrifice. Christian life should then be a struggle, until the strategy of Jesus triumphs and itself becomes evolutionarily stable.

What does our study of the culture of sacrifice have to do with our examination of the five commandments of Jesus? Two things:

First, our study shows that the areas in which the five commandments are to be practiced include not only the sphere of personal life and action but also the public, social, and institutional sphere. As we saw in Chapter 2, the five commandments of Jesus are quite specifically directed at the four naturally selected genetically based anti-social human behaviors of violence, acquisitiveness, kinship affinity, and dominant-submissive behaviors. As we've seen in this chapter, the power of the dominant culture of the world, the culture of sacrifice, the "powers that be," is based on the absorption, channeling, and internalization of these genetically based behaviors into human social, political, and economic institutions. The five commandments of Jesus are thus specifically directed toward the reform and renovation of these institutions. We'll examine in detail how and under what conditions the five commandments should be applied to the public sphere in Chapter 8.

Second, we've seen that the institution of human sacrifice itself, or the scapegoating sacrifice, is central to the culture of sacrifice and thus to the injustices absorbed into and embedded in its public institutions. As Jesus opposed defective and unjust public institutions – "I testify to it that its works are evil"; "Now the ruler of this world will be driven out" – so he also opposed human sacrifice itself. We'll see in greater detail just how he opposed the institution of human sacrifice, and how he overthrew it, in Chapters 5 and 6.

Jesus intended his five commandments to be the means by which not only individual lives, but the whole world, would be changed and redeemed. As the author of the Gospel of John puts it, "God sent not his Son into the world to condemn the world; but that the world through him might be saved" (Jn 3:17). This makes the five commandments of Jesus very important indeed.

We now take a short break from historical, anthropological, and cultural matters, for some theological reflections.

Notes and Sources for Further Reading

Girard's theory of sacrifice is set forth in his *Violence and the Sacred* (Johns Hopkins University Press, 1977); *Things Hidden Since the Foundation of the World* (Stanford University Press, 1987); and *The Scapegoat* (Johns Hopkins University Press, 1986). I am deeply indebted to Girard for this theory. I suggest that the curious reader start with *Things Hidden*.

The Legend of the North Star is found in Joseph Campbell's *Historical Atlas of World Mythology* (Harper & Row, 1988), Vol. II, Part 2, p. 177.

The concept of evolutionary stability is found in Robert Axelrod's book, *The Evolution of Cooperation* (Basic Books, 1984), Chapters 3 and 5.

The religions of Rome are described in Keith Hopkins's book, *A World Full of Gods* (Penguin Putnam, 2001), an amusing and very informative book.

The discussion of lynching in America is based on Philip Dray's *At the Hands of Persons Unknown: The Lynching of Black America* (Random House, 2002). The quotation (with emphasis added) is from p. 79.

The discussion of historic Christian ethical teaching is based on Daniel Harrington's and James F. Keenan's book, *Jesus and Virtue Ethics: Building Bridges Between New Testament Studies and Moral Theology* (Rowman & Littlefield, 2002). The quotation is from p. 3.

Walter Wink's book, *Engaging the Powers* (Fortress Press, 1992), is a particularly good introduction to the study of social sin, the "powers that be," as is his shorter version of that book, called *The Powers That Be* (Galilee Doubleday, 1998).

IV

The Dilemma of the Genetically Based Behaviors

"And you will know the truth, and the truth will set you free." (Jn 8:32)

AFTER MY PERCEPTIVE NEPHEW MARK read the first three chapters of this book in draft, he pointed out to me that my description of the genetically based anti-social behaviors in Chapter 2, and their development and internalization in human institutions in Chapter 3, raises a theological dilemma: If God created the world and humanity as we know it, God created a world in which humanity would evolve from lower animals. These genetically based behaviors developed in animals prior to the evolution of humans and are found in all of us, even the earliest humans. Thus God, not humanity, is responsible for their presence in us. Yet evil consequences flow from their presence in us, and, as we saw in the first chapter, Jesus repeatedly and consistently preached that these behaviors must be resisted and overcome.

Was God wrong or mistaken when he gave humanity these genetically based behaviors? Is God implicated in the sins and evils which have been committed by us humans in whom these behaviors are genetically based? And did God then change his mind when he inspired Jesus to preach against them? We need to find an explanation which permits us to answer these questions in the negative, or we will be stuck with a highly imperfect and changeable God, not the Father of whom Jesus spoke, and not the Christian God.

One way to avoid this dilemma is to accept the traditional Jewish and Christian account of the creation and fall of humans. According to the story of Adam and Eve in the first three chapters of Genesis, and according to the Christian doctrine of original sin based on that story, humanity was created, in the persons of Adam and Eve, in a state of sinless perfection. They and their descendants were destined to pass into eternal blessedness without death. God tested Adam and Eve by giving them a command, a trivial rule of dietary restriction, and they failed the test. Because of their disobedience, all humanity was separated from God and punished by God with travail and suffering during life and with death at the end.

According to this doctrine, all of us have inherited this sin of Adam and Eve, called the "original sin." One consequence of this is that all of us have inclinations toward bad conduct. Another consequence, held to be true by many Christian denominations, is that none of us are capable of doing any act which has merit before God unless and until we are baptized as Christians or accept Jesus as Lord and Savior. In some Christian denominations, even baptized Christians remain incapable of doing any act which has merit before God. Jesus came to save us, or redeem us, from this original sin and its effects.

This doctrine preserves God from any association with or implication in human evil and sin and from being implicated in natural evils (flood, fire, earthquake, etc.) as well. It's close to, but different from, the Manichaean teachings (based on ancient Zoroastrian teachings) which avoid the dilemma the same way, by holding that there are two gods, one good god, who created humanity, and one evil god, who causes or incites all the evil in this world, and that these two gods will contest with each other for dominion over humanity until the end of time. Augustine (354-430), the great Christian theologian of the patristic period, is principally responsible for developing in full the traditional doctrines of original sin and of the resulting innate depravity of humans. It's worth noting that he had been a Manichaean before he became a Christian.

There's one true and accurate observation in the traditional Christian doctrine of original sin: all of us have inclinations, difficult to resist and control, toward evil conduct, and all of us at one time or another actually do succumb to these inclinations and do evil things to our fellow humans. This is certain. We all have inclinations to evil, and the genetically based anti-social behaviors are only part, although the most stubborn part, of them.

The rest of the doctrine of original sin can't stand in the face of critical examination. To list just a few of the critical objections to the traditional doctrine:

1.   God didn't in fact create humanity in a state of sinless perfection, without suffering or death. All paleontology and cultural anthropology, and all evolutionary biology, including that discussed in Chapter 2, is to the contrary.

2.   In the Genesis myth, Adam and Eve were far from perfect; they were hopelessly naive and adolescent. We can't imagine any kind of original perfection of humanity without immunity from, or at least strong powers of resistance against, temptation to sin of any kind. But we find none of that in Adam and Eve. One word from the serpent, and they ate the fruit. What the text of Genesis supports isn't the fall of mankind. What the text shows is that prior to the fall, Adam and Eve were all too fallible and human and their trust in God and in God's word was shallow and fickle. We can all identify with the vulnerability of Adam and Eve to temptation, because, in the Genesis myth itself, human nature is shown to be exactly the same before the "fall" as it was afterward. In other words, there was no "fall," and Adam's sin wasn't the "original sin." Vulnerability to temptation, travail and suffering during life, and death at the end have always been part of the human condition.

3.   The doctrine of original sin depends on the assertion that the guilt and punishment for the disobedience of one pair of humans was and is to be borne by all humans. This is profoundly unjust, pernicious and unscientific. It's unjust, because the relationship between each of us and a benevolent God is, and must be, ultimately up to each of us and God. This relationship can't in justice be changed by the conduct of two people far away in a strange land thousands of years ago. It's pernicious, because it teaches that men and women can be held responsible for, and can be punished for, the sins of their ancestors. This has often been used as a powerful rationalization for inter-ethnic, inter-religious, and inter-racial prejudice and persecution. For example, Jews born after the death of Jesus can't possibly be held responsible for his death; but many of them have been persecuted on that account.

The doctrine of original sin is also contrary to science. The doctrine asserts that the acts of one person affect the genetic inheritance of that person's progeny. This is faulty biology. No information about the activities of a person during his or her life, or about that person's acquired character, can be transmitted from that person's body or mind to the genetic material which that person transmits to his or her offspring. This is the central dogma of molecular biology. Modern science has definitively concluded that sin and guilt can't pass from generation to generation.

4.   The doctrine of original sin implies that the redemptive activity of Jesus was directed toward changing *God's* attitude toward humanity, turning aside his wrath, satisfying his need for justice, and so on, rather than toward changing *humanity's* attitudes and human acts, particularly in the most harmful and intractable areas of human conduct. But this is neither what Jesus did, nor what he said he came to do. Jesus said, "I must proclaim the good news of the kingdom of God to the other cities also; *for I was sent for this purpose*" (Lk 4:43). The view that the redemptive activity of Jesus was directed toward God, rather than toward us humans, can only be held if (a) we ignore the teachings, particularly the ethical teachings, of Jesus, and concentrate exclusively on his death, and if (b) we then misconstrue the death of Jesus as a blood sacrifice to appease God's harsh justice and wrath, ignoring the fact that a blood sacrifice is and always has been an abhorrent act, an act of violence and murder concealed by lies and self-deception.

If we reject the Adam and Eve story as myth, and conclude that the doctrine of original sin is untenable, as I do, and if we accept the fact that much human evil arises from the genetically based anti-social behaviors and their absorption into human institutions, as I do, we must find a different explanation to reconcile the presence of these behaviors in humans with the idea of a benevolent and loving creator God. I've found three different ways of resolving the dilemma, or three aspects of one explanation for why we have these behaviors, which involve three progressively deeper levels of consideration.

First Reflection: The genetically based behaviors were necessary for survival of the original humans and don't go away when we no longer need them for that purpose.

The naturally selected behaviors of violence, kinship affinity, dominant-submissive behaviors, and acquisitiveness were survival skills for primitive humans, as they were for the primates from which humans emerged. That's why they were naturally selected: they gave their possessors increased abilities to survive and reproduce in a hostile "survival of the fittest" environment. They were essential components of the emergence of humanity from the lower animals. When, then, did they become problems? They became problems for humans only after humans began forming social and economic communities larger than the tribe or clan. Why didn't they then evolve to meet human cultural development? Because human culture and human social and economic institutions arise and change much more rapidly than genetic changes can take place. Even if there were any reason to believe that the instinctive anti-social behaviors of humans would change by natural selection (which there isn't), the required changes would fall very far behind the changing needs of humans. The only way in which the evil effects of these instinctive behaviors can be resisted and overcome is with personal resistance and with cultural and institutional changes, and that's what Jesus taught us should be done when he preached his five commandments.

Second Reflection: The genetically based behaviors are thoroughly combined with and inseparable from essential human virtues, without which we wouldn't be human.

I've followed the evolutionary psychologists in identifying and discussing four genetically based anti-social behaviors and the cultural anthropologists in showing how human societies have controlled these behaviors by channeling and internalizing them in human institutions rather than by resisting and opposing them. Identification of these behaviors for analytical purposes ignores the fact that in real human life each of these behaviors is an aspect, a dangerous aspect, of an integrated pattern of human behavior which is, for the most part, both good in itself and necessary for human life and growth. Let's look at these behaviors one by one:

Violence, particularly male violence, is closely related to the human ambition to perform great deeds, the drive to excel, the desire to accomplish our will in action. The desire for revenge is in part a desire for justice and is close to the desire to protect and defend ourselves and our kin. While we deplore the violence of the warrior, we would not want to lose the valor and the heroism which courageous men and women muster to overcome difficult challenges. The urge to do violence is related to the courage needed to persevere in any difficult task and to the willingness, if needed, to lay down our life for the life of another human being.

The fear, suspicion, and hatred of strangers which arises out of kinship affinity, or out of excessive solidarity with any identity group, is the destructive aspect of the virtues of loyalty to, and wholehearted participation in, the activities of any identity group. Kinship affinity is the emotional bond which holds together the family, the school, the church, and the nation. Without it, parents wouldn't care for their children or for their aged relatives.

Dominant-submissive behaviors are often the inappropriate extensions of proper parent-child relationship patterns into inter-adult relationship patterns. These behaviors are also closely related to the virtues of respect for proper authority and respect for professional skills and competence. Leaders are needed for human social and cultural groups of all kinds, and the functioning of any group requires a willingness to work within its structure, whether simple or elaborate, to get along and to get things done.

A certain amount of acquisitiveness is needed to acquire life's necessities, food, drink, clothing, and shelter, and to provide for their continued supply during the times of year when ready food isn't available and shelter from bad weather is needed. What Jesus emphasized in his fifth commandment wasn't absolute poverty, but putting work for the growth of the kingdom of God ahead of work for possessions.

It's difficult or impossible to imagine what human life would be like without our ambition and courage to pursue excellence and competence, without parental and familial mutual care and love, without leadership in human social or group activities, or without responsible foresight and provision for our own material needs and those of our family. It's difficult to imagine what kind of beings God would have created if she had assured that those beings would not lack these virtues, but would not be troubled by violence, kinship affinity, dominant-submissive behaviors, and acquisitiveness. If she had done so, such beings would not be like us or like the human beings we know.

It's even harder to imagine anything resembling human life which doesn't begin, for each one of us, with birth. Each human life begins with a baby, primitive, unformed, without culture or morals, and without institutions of any kind except the immediate family. Each of us must learn, starting in early childhood, by trial and error, how to control our own bodies, our own emotions, and our own desires. Each of us must learn from our earliest years what to desire, mostly by learning what to desire from others, and then each of us must learn to deal with the conflict situations to which these imitative or mimetic desires very frequently lead.

The presence of the instinctive genetically based anti-social behaviors and human growth from infancy to maturity are clearly an integral part of what humanity is. We must conclude that they are part of the package which makes us human and are inseparable from the rest. God could have done it differently, but that would be a different species of being in a different kind of world.

> *Third Reflection: All of human life and freedom requires developing self-control and learning general and special competencies by practice against resistance. The genetically based behaviors are just part, if the most difficult part, of the resistance against which we must practice.*

A commonly-held outlook on life, among Christians and non Christians alike, is that we are born into a world of known rules and required behaviors, which direct us toward good actions and away from evil actions. Those of us who learn and follow the rules consistently are good people and good citizens. For people of a religious faith, there may be more rules, but those rules are also known, and the consequences of following those rules are not only good citizenship but salvation. We each feel from time to time a desire to do what we should avoid, and our freedom, our capacity to choose between good and evil, is what makes it possible for us to turn toward evil conduct. Good conduct means living by the rules and following them faithfully. Sometimes it seems that we'd all be better off if we didn't have the freedom to break the rules and endanger our salvation. But that's a poor notion of human freedom. Let's take a broader and more fundamental view of what it means to be free, by considering human aspirations.

There is in every one of us a personal principle of freedom, which is the desire and need to determine for ourselves what we aspire to be, and to do, and then to succeed in realizing our chosen goals. Everyone also desires to love and to be loved, and we can use our freedom to realize this goal, because true freedom includes the ability to reach out effectively and lovingly to others. Self-directed action which is effective and helpful to others is true freedom. Those of us who are able to exercise effective self-direction are mature, and have developed individuality and character.

We all aspire to the true, the good, and the beautiful. We seek the power and the ability to see and to express new and meaningful truths about the world, about humans, and about everything. We want to love well, to do justice, and to work with our brothers and our sisters to build good societies and institutions. We want certainly to appreciate, and possibly to create, beauty in all its forms: literature, painting, music, dance; and to share our appreciations and our creations with each other. We all desire and need to grow and develop our freedom so that we can choose and achieve these goals.

What does it take to achieve and share true freedom, freedom of competence and accomplishment? It seems to me that it takes two things: first, the development from within of control of our desires and actions, and second, the acquisition of competencies and skills. In childhood and adolescence, we learn basic self-control, and we acquire basic competencies: language, social skills, and some familiarity with our history, the sciences of the world, and computational skills. In adolescence and adulthood, we enlarge and refine our social skills and general competencies, and we acquire one or more specialized competencies, so we can make a living, contribute to society, and appreciate the good things of life. In every case, learning self-control and acquiring any competency, basic or specialized, requires regular and diligent practice against resistance. Only with practice against resistance do we develop good habits and expand our abilities; only with practice against resistance do we become free.

In one of his letters, John Stuart Mill expressed this imperative for human life:

> There is only one plain rule of life eternally binding, and independent of all variations in creeds and in the interpretation of creeds and embracing equally the greatest moralities and the smallest – it is this – try thyself unweariedly till thou findest the highest thing thou are capable of doing, faculties and outward circumstances being both duly considered – and then DO IT!

The goal of every one of us should thus be to marry our professional, trade, and domestic competencies to our desires to help others. In this way we'll exercise true freedom and creativity and advance the work of the kingdom.

In the course of becoming free persons, we choose, and each choice limits our subsequent choices. If I choose to study law (as I did), I thereby foreclose any opportunities to be a carpenter, a professional musician or a doctor. If I choose one woman to be my wife (as I did), I thereby foreclose intimate relations with other women. But each foreclosure also increases my freedom in real and practical ways. Only if I study law with dedication and intensity can I actually help others by counseling them in legal matters. Only if I choose a wife can I have a relationship of committed love to her, and to a family. The Latin American Jesuit theologian Juan Luis Segundo puts it this way:

> If . . . freedom consists in making one's own being into a creation that springs from our inmost depths, then the active (not passive) elimination of the possibility of choosing is something positive. To love — the creative action *par excellence* — is deliberately to choose to lose one's own autonomy. To do this, however, *we must use and channel the forces that are within us at the start as instinctive forces.*
> Consider sex, for example. For the vast majority of human beings, freedom from egoistic and passive solipsism is possible only insofar as self-giving utilizes the sexual instinct. In other words, a person frees himself by stripping sex of its merely instinctive character and converting it into what it really is: a vehicle of personalization and hence of human community. Love will use the basic instinct of sex for self-giving.

True freedom is difficult to attain, and, once attained, it's difficult to maintain. Freedom is chosen, and it must be chosen constantly. The opposition to freedom isn't positively chosen bad conduct; it's going with the flow, taking it easy, slacking off, and accepting without critical reflection the rules and customs of our social milieu. These rules and customs are part of the resistance against which we must practice. In a paradoxical way, yielding to whatever views prevail at any given time is retreating into egoism by declining to be self-directed. As Segundo puts it, "Man can turn his freedom into just another thing: dominated, alienated, predictable, echoing alien thoughts, and passively submitting to the impact of society."

In a way, the rules and customs of traditional Christian churches are part of the problem, not part of the solution. As we saw in Chapter 3, and will see again, the nations and cultures of the world have internalized the genetically based behaviors of violence, kinship affinity, dominant-submissive relationships, and acquisitiveness. Traditional Christianity has rarely said anything about this. The general outlook of the Christian churches, understood if not articulated, has been the outlook described at the beginning of this section: the rules include the laws of the government as well as the rules and customs of the church, and the good Christian obeys these laws and follows these rules and customs.

But this is the abdication of true personal freedom in matters in the public sphere. To be fully free, we need to study critically the laws and institutions of church and society and oppose rules and customs which institutionalize the genetically based anti-social behaviors. In Chapter 8, I'll show how opposition to these behaviors, by application of the five commandments of Jesus, can be put into practice. For the present, let me simply observe how the presence of the genetically based behaviors in ourselves and in our social and political institutions relates to human freedom.

If freedom, as I've described it, is among our truest goals; if we attain freedom, like all of our capabilities, only by struggle, by practice against resistance; and if we are not wholly self-centered and autonomous individuals, but must work together to achieve any common good, then the presence of the genetically based behaviors in ourselves and in our institutions is a good thing. It puts our social and political institutions in play, not as makers of rules to be followed, but as institutions to be reformed, so that all humans may be free. The genetically based behaviors in human institutions are an important part of the resistance against which we must practice. Segundo puts it this way:

> Each person's path to freedom . . . . takes concrete form *when the person shoulders the task of moving from an established morality that he or she did not choose to a creative morality involving the formulation of a new societal scheme,* and when then the person engages in action to transform the structures which are perpetuating his or her alienation. In short, freedom is practically manifested in ideological transformation and political action.

Throughout history, successful free men and women have chosen what they have wished to do, and they have done it, by developing self-control and social skills and practicing in their arts and sciences against the resistance of the inherent difficulties of the subject matter, the distractions of frivolous pursuits, waste of time and indolence, and the unreflective acceptance of all the rules and customs of society. But free men and women have always needed, in addition, a social structure which gives them space and opportunity to engage in and develop their arts, sciences, crafts, and skills.

Over the course of history, successful societies have created this space and opportunity for free men and women by organizing reasonably well-administered states, with settled laws and customs, and by providing, in one way or another, for public safety. But to create the space for their own privileged classes, most societies have dealt with some of their most difficult problems by putting their problems outside the privileged space – that is, by externalizing them. Violence has been dealt with by externalizing it in wars against outsiders and in confinement or exile of the society's own criminal and dissident classes. Kinship affinity has been dealt with by identifying all within the nation as a kinship group and all others as outsiders. Hierarchies have been formed to protect the freedom and space of the privileged classes against the laboring classes and the poor. Wealth has been concentrated among the few for the same purpose. Within these arrangements, the creativity and industry of the free men (and sometimes women) of such societies has been able to flourish. Think of ancient Athens or of the Italian city-states of the Renaissance.

But now the world is too small for this. We are now too close to our fellow citizens of the world, and our freedom now depends to no small extent on theirs. Human society now requires an effort to deal with the genetically based anti-social behaviors by resisting and opposing them, not externalizing them, because externalizing our problems no longer works. It's now necessary to reform the institutions and change the rules and customs by which the consequences of these behaviors are directed toward outsiders, because in this world there are no longer outsiders, and we can't continue with customs, cultures, and institutional practices which separate humans from one another.

How will we do this? By applying our own freedom and creativity to understanding these problems; by developing habits of resistance to the genetically based anti-social behaviors in our personal lives; by finding practical ways to remove defects from the customs and the culture of society, and practical reforms for our institutions; and then by developing the basic and the specialized competencies we need to address these problems and make the needed changes in the human way, by persistent and disciplined exercise of these competencies against resistance. The best way to do this, it seems to me, is to study, practice, and apply the five commandments of Jesus in our own lives and in the world.

In principle, then, the creation of humanity with genetically based anti-social behaviors isn't different from the creation of humanity with periods of infancy, childhood, adolescence, maturity, and old age in each life, or the creation of humanity with an absence of inborn or intuitive competencies in all the arts, sciences, crafts, and skills which civilization requires or permits. In each case, the task and response of men and women like you and me who wish to achieve true freedom in action as well as in thought and word is to develop self-control and social skills, to learn general competencies, and to master the specialized competencies of our freely chosen fields by continuous, diligent, and lifelong practice against resistance. This certainly appears to be what God created us to do.

The genetically based anti-social behaviors and their absorption within human institutions are part of God's plan. We were made to grow in strength, knowledge, power, and love by our own free efforts with practice against resistance. God gave us the resistance against which to practice, and the genetically based behaviors are part, but only part, of that resistance.

Whether the presence in all humans of the genetically based anti-social behavior patterns required a redemptive intervention by God is another question. There are two principal indications that it did:

1.   The history of civilizations and our observations about the present situation of humanity suggest strongly that the internalization of these genetically based behaviors by human societies and institutions has reached evolutionary stability, as I proposed in Chapter 3. It can't correct itself from within.

2.   The facts of the life, teaching, death, and resurrection of Jesus indicate that Jesus himself thought his mission was a public intervention by God in human civilization. Jesus directed the bulk of his new and different ethical teachings, his five commandments, against the

genetically based behaviors and in favor of the habits and behaviors by which they would eventually, he thought, be overcome. Jesus clearly intended, with his five commandments in particular, to change the way humans thought, felt, and acted toward one another. It clearly never occurred to him that he was in any way going to change God's attitude toward humans. The sayings of Jesus about what following his five commandments will entail show not only his respect and understanding for the freedom of men and women to follow him, or not, and his empathy with his followers about the difficulties of following his teachings, but also his firm conviction that following his teachings is necessary.

Conclusion. On the basis of these reflections, we can give negative answers to the questions asked in the second paragraph of this chapter.

1.   God was not mistaken when she gave humanity the genetically based anti-social behaviors. Learning self-control and control of our desires, our emotions, and these behaviors is part of the essence of what it means to be human. It's what we do and how we live and mature.

2.   God is no more and no less implicated in the sins and evils which flow from the genetically based behaviors than she is in the sins and evils which flow from human desires, human immaturity, and human freedom generally. If God is God, she will judge each of us fairly, because she knows each of us better than any of us knows himself or herself. And, as Jesus taught, God is always gratuitously generous and forgiving.

3.   God didn't change her mind when she inspired Jesus to preach radical resistance to the genetically based behaviors. They and the teachings of Jesus against them are both part of God's plan for humanity. One consequence of the presence of both the anti-social behaviors and the mission of Jesus is that God's plan obviously requires that men and women work together in groups to preserve, practice, and spread implementation of the five commandments of Jesus. This is the Christian church, and it too is part of the plan.

After this short theological interlude, we return to the story of Jesus: some of his religious and doctrinal teachings, and his death and resurrection.

Notes and Sources for Further Reading

An excellent book on original sin, with contemporary analysis, is Tatha Wiley's *Original Sin* (Paulist Press, 2002).

For an explanation of the concept of evolutionary stability, see Robert Axelrod's *The Evolution of Cooperation* (Basic Books, 1984), Chapters 3 and 5.

John Stuart Mill's letter is found in Richard Reeves's *John Stuart Mill: Victorian Firebrand* (Atlantic Books, London, 2007), p. 157.

I am indebted to Juan Luis Segundo for his brilliant description of human freedom, set forth in his book, *Grace and the Human Condition* (Orbis Books, 1973). The quotations (emphasis added) are from pages 159, 43 and 39 respectively.

V

The Kingdom and the End of Sacrifice

"I am the vine, you are the branches." (Jn 15:5)

WE'VE SEEN THAT THE FIVE COMMANDMENTS OF JESUS are directed with precision against the genetically based anti-social behaviors of human beings. We've seen that the prevailing culture of the world, the culture of sacrifice, which has its roots in the practice of human sacrifice, channeled these genetically based behaviors and internalized them in the institutions of society. Thus the five commandments of Jesus are precisely directed not only against these behaviors in individuals, but also against these behaviors in social, cultural, and political institutions, customs, and practices.

So far, we've studied only the teachings of Jesus which set forth and illustrate the five commandments themselves. We now turn to two other bodies of teachings of Jesus: his teachings about the kingdom of God and his attack on the elements of the culture of sacrifice. Both of these bodies of teaching show us how the five commandments of Jesus are only the central thrust of Jesus's broad-based and integrated assault on the genetically based behaviors and the culture in which they are imbedded. They show us Jesus's vision of what must be changed, what must be put in its place, and how Jesus foresees that this is to happen.

The Kingdom of God.

Jesus spent a lot of time and energy preaching about the coming of the kingdom of God (which the writer of Matthew calls the kingdom of heaven). Unfortunately, Jesus never explained what the kingdom of God is in direct language, as far as we know. He either used the term without explanation or described the kingdom in similes or parables. The thirteenth chapter of Matthew alone contains eight different similes or parables describing the kingdom: the kingdom of heaven is like a mustard seed; like yeast; like treasure hidden in a field; like a merchant in search of fine pearls; like a net thrown into the sea.

The result is that nobody seems to have a clear idea of what the kingdom of God is, or how it is to work. Some scholars and writers think that the kingdom of God is what happens at the end of days, when God comes to rule as a king. Others think that Jesus meant that the time of the kingdom was the time in which he was living and teaching. Some think the kingdom is in heaven, as in "Blessed are the poor in spirit, for theirs is the kingdom of heaven" (Mt 5:3; Lk 6:20). Others think the kingdom is, or will be, on earth, as in "Blessed are the meek, for they will inherit the earth" (Mt 5:5). Some think the establishment of the kingdom will be the work of God alone, and we humans are to be passive observers. Others think the kingdom is something which men and women like us will participate in creating. The five commandments of Jesus shed some light on these questions and help explain what Jesus meant by the kingdom of God; and the idea of the kingdom, so clarified, in turn sheds additional light on the working out of the five commandments.

Let's start with the most well-known saying of Jesus about the kingdom of God, the phrase in the Lord's Prayer, "Thy kingdom come" (Mt 6:10; Lk 11:2). The immediately following phrase, "Thy will be done on earth as it is in heaven" (Mt 6:10), occurs only in Matthew's version of the Lord's Prayer, and (except for a very few manuscripts) not in Luke's version. Because of this, many scholars have concluded that the phrase "Thy will be done on earth as it is in heaven" was probably added by Matthew, or by someone in the Matthew tradition, and is probably not an actual saying of Jesus.

The substance of the phrase is certainly consistent with the teachings of Jesus. He regarded all of his teaching as the teaching of God's will, and he clearly hoped, and urged us to pray, that God's will would be followed, would be "done on earth." But why did the Matthew tradition add this phrase at this point? It doesn't effect a change of meaning, but simply an expansion of the phrase "Thy kingdom come." I suggest that this is exactly what was intended: the additional phrase is an explanation of or definition of the kingdom. The two phrases could (and, in my view, should) be read, "Thy kingdom come; *that is to say,* thy will be done on earth as it is in heaven."

The kingdom of God thus comes as and when God's will is done on earth as it is in heaven. If this is so, what does it imply?

First, it means that God's will must be a set of instructions or commands for action, not simply for belief; God's will is to be "done," or acted upon, not simply believed.

Second, it's Jesus's view that God is remote ("Our Father who art in heaven") and does not announce his will separately, but through Jesus, who is here as God's representative. Jesus clearly believes that the message he is bringing to the world is God's will mediated to humanity through him. As we saw in the first chapter, the central prescriptions for action contained in the teachings of Jesus are the teachings we've called his five commandments. Jesus clearly regarded them as God's will – "the word that you hear is not mine, but is from the Father who sent me" (Jn 14:24). Thus the kingdom comes as and when the five commandments are practiced.

Third, Jesus addressed the five commandments to men and women. He didn't ask God to live by them; he told us to live by them. We're not meant to be passive about the coming of the kingdom of God. We're not simply to wait for the coming of a king who will put all things right. We're intended to bring the kingdom of God to the world by our own human efforts, as and when we follow the five commandments of Jesus and apply them in our own lives and to the institutions of the world.

There's an obviously antiquated part of the concept of the kingdom of God, which is the notion of kingship itself. The popular Christian understanding of the kingdom of God, which we find in hymns and prayers in every Christian church, seems to be that in the last days, Jesus will return to the earth and rule as its universal king. In other words, while we now have a preference for representative democracy (and indeed, to some American politicians, a divine mission to spread representative democracy around the world), God has a preference for a kingdom over which Jesus will rule with the powers of an absolute monarch. He will decide, as king, whether we will have single-payer universal health insurance and which highways and bridges will be built or repaired with public funds. It doesn't occur to American Christians that this belief in a coming divine monarchy runs counter to the basic point of the Declaration of Independence as well as to the lasting legacy of the Magna Carta.

This can't be the meaning of the kingdom of God. For one thing, the fundamental meaning of salvation is the realization of the freedom and creativity of all men and women. Reducing us from the status of citizens to the status of subjects and taking all responsibility for public decisions away from us is hardly consistent with increasing our freedom and creativity. For another, it demeans the teaching of Jesus to think that he was expressing a preference for one form of political system over another. I think most Christians share this view, and so most Christians don't think about the kingdom of God very often, if at all.

When Jesus talked about the "kingdom," he was simply using the only term available, in the common language of the time, to describe an organized and united community. So I think that the kingdom of God must be taken to mean simply some kind of organized and governed community of men and women. In our time, we would expect such a community, if it claimed to be a just and moral community of free men and women, to be self-governed in some way. It would not be a kingdom, and it would not have a king.

What then would be the organizing principle of such a community, if not monarchy? Surely a set of laws, just and moral laws. And if the community is meant to be universal, as Jesus surely indicated, the laws should be trans-cultural. A set of laws or commandments directed against the anti-social tendencies all humans have in common, because the tendencies are found in the human genome, would surely be an appropriate choice. This seems to support the conclusion reached in our discussion of the Lord's Prayer: that the kingdom of God, as Jesus used the term, is and will be the community of men and women who follow and observe the five commandments of Jesus.

If this conclusion is sound, the kingdom of God began when Jesus first taught his five commandments. The public activities of Jesus at that point in time had consisted solely of his preaching and healing. Did Jesus speak then about the kingdom of God as already present? Yes, he did. Jesus began his ministry with the words, "The time is fulfilled, and the kingdom of God has come near" (Mk 1:15; Mt 4:17). When Jesus was accused of casting out demons by Beelzebul (a devil), he answered his accusers that "If it is by the finger of God that I cast out demons, then the kingdom of God has come to you" (Lk 11:20; Mt 12:28). When the Pharisees asked him when the kingdom of God was coming, his answer was "In fact, the kingdom of God is in your midst" (Lk 17:21).

When Jesus first preached the five commandments, the kingdom began. But there were as yet only hearers; there was no body or group which had begun to live by the five commandments. Whatever kind of movement would grow out of the teachings of Jesus, it hadn't then begun to grow; it was only a seed. Jesus used this precise metaphor in the parable of the sower and his seed (Mt 13:3-23; Mk 4:3-20; Lk 8:5-15):

> Listen! A sower went out to sow. And as he sowed, some seeds fell on the path, and the birds came and ate them up. Other seeds fell on rocky ground, where they did not have much soil, and they sprang up quickly, since they had no depth of soil. But when the sun rose, they were scorched; and since they had no root, they withered away. Other seeds fell among thorns, and the thorns grew up and choked them. Other seeds fell on good soil and brought forth grain, some a hundredfold, some sixty, some thirty. Let anyone with ears listen!

The disciples, never very swift, didn't understand. Jesus explained the parable to them, saying, "When anyone hears the word of the kingdom and does not understand it, the evil one comes and snatches away what is sown in the heart; this is what was sown on the path." And he continued to explain the parable, clearly identifying the seed with the word, or the commandments, of the kingdom. (As I pointed out in the first chapter, Jesus often used "word" and "commandments" interchangeably.)

Again, using the same metaphor, Jesus taught the parable of the wheat and the weeds (Mt 13:24-30):

> The kingdom of heaven may be compared to someone who sowed good seed in his field; but while everybody was asleep, an enemy came and sowed weeds among the wheat, and then went away. So when the plants came up and bore grain, then the weeds appeared as well. And the servants of the householder came to him and said to him, "Master, did you not sow good seed in your field? Where, then, did these weeds come from?" He answered, "An enemy has done this." The servants said to him, "Then do you want us to go and gather them?" But he replied, "No; for in gathering the weeds you would uproot the wheat along with them. Let both of them grow together until the harvest; and at harvest time I will tell the reapers, collect the weeds first and bind them in bundles to be burned, but gather the wheat into my barn."

Later, his disciples asked for an explanation of this parable. Jesus explained, "The one who sows the good seed is the Son of Man [Jesus's term for himself], the field is the world, and the good seed are the children of the kingdom" (Mt 13:37-38). It seems to me that a natural and fair interpretation of this sentence is, "The one who teaches the five commandments is the Son of Man, the field is the world, and the community of men and women who practice the five commandments are the children of the kingdom."

The kingdom would grow over time, Jesus asserted:

> The kingdom of heaven is like a mustard seed that someone took and sowed in his field; it is the smallest of all the seeds, but when it has grown it is the greatest of shrubs and becomes a tree, so that the birds of the air come and make nests in its branches. . . . The kingdom of heaven is like yeast that a woman took and mixed in with three measures of flour until all of it was leavened. (Mt 13:31-33; Lk 13:18-20)

As yeast changes the whole bread, the kingdom of God will change the world. And, like the mustard seed growing over many years into a tree, or like bread slowly rising after the yeast is added to the flour, the kingdom of God will grow slowly and gradually over time through natural, not magical, processes. The obvious implication is that if and when communities of men and women follow and practice the five commandments of Jesus, the world will be changed.

This view of the idea of the kingdom of God, as Jesus used the term, isn't exclusive. But I suggest that it presents a good way of interpreting Jesus's parables and of understanding some of what he was trying to say. The "seed" of the kingdom of God is the central ethical teaching of Jesus, his five commandments. The kingdom will grow from the seed and bear fruit as and when men and women, together in communities, practice his five commandments. And the kingdom of God will eventually triumph over the culture of sacrifice, "so that the birds of the air will come and make nests in its branches" and so that all the bread will be leavened.

Attacking the Elements of Sacrifice.

Jesus attacked the culture of sacrifice not only with his teaching of his five commandments, which counseled radical resistance to the foundations of that culture, but also with direct attacks on the sacrifice itself, the source and center of that culture, and on the elements of sacrificial culture. There had grown up around the ancient sacrifice an elaborate set of rules, rituals, and practices, all as means to preserve the magical sacredness of the sacrificial rites: holy days, holy places, ritual cleanness, dietary purity, rules of shunning those not worthy to participate in the sacrifice, and practices of public and ostentatious prayer and fasting. Jesus systematically attacked all of these rules and practices. Let's take them one by one:

Jesus went out of his way to flout the rules of observance of the Sabbath as then taught and practiced in Israel. He deliberately incurred the anger and hostility of the scribes and Pharisees in doing so. On one occasion, Jesus and his disciples were in a grain field on the Sabbath, and his disciples, being hungry, plucked the grain and ate it. The Pharisees told Jesus that what his disciples were doing was not lawful on the Sabbath. Jesus defended his disciples, cited precedent in the law, and concluded by saying, "The Sabbath was made for humankind, and not humankind for the Sabbath; so the Son of Man is Lord even of the Sabbath" (Mk 2:23-28; Mt 12:1-8; Lk 6:1-5).

Jesus is reported to have performed no fewer than five miracles of healing on the Sabbath, in each case in the face of the opposition and hostility of the Jewish religious establishment: a man with a withered hand (Mk 3:1-6; Mt 12:9-14; Lk 6:6-11); a woman who had been crippled for eighteen years (Lk 13:10-17); a man with dropsy (Lk 14:1-6); a man who had been an invalid for thirty-eight years (Jn 5:2-18); and a man born blind (Jn 9:1-41). One would think that, if keeping the Sabbath was important, or even acceptable, to him, he could have asked the man who had been an invalid for thirty-eight years, or the man born blind, to wait until Sunday. But Jesus wanted to make a point. Preceding two of these cures (the man with the withered hand and the man with dropsy), he challenged the observing Pharisees, asking whether it was lawful to cure on the Sabbath. On both occasions his question was met with stony silence. In all five of the cure narratives it is reported that the Jewish religious leaders subsequently condemned his actions. In two of the cure narratives it is reported that they then plotted to kill him.

In Paul's epistle to the Galatians, Paul broadens this rule beyond the Sabbath alone: "You are observing special days, and months, and seasons, and years. I am afraid that my work for you may have been wasted" (Gal 4:10-11).   So much for the calendar of feasts in the Christian churches!

Jesus said that there are no longer to be sacred places for worship. To the Samaritan woman at the well, he said, "Woman, believe me, the hour is coming when you will worship the Father neither on this mountain nor in Jerusalem. . . . True worshipers will worship the Father in spirit and truth" (Jn 4:21, 23).   And he rather dramatically and forcefully interrupted religious and sacrificial proceedings at the Temple in Jerusalem (Mt 21:12-13; Mk 11:15-17; Lk 19:45-46; Jn 2:13-16).

Jesus regularly defied the Jewish rules of ritual cleanness. The scribes and Pharisees asked him why his disciples had broken ritual cleanness by eating with unwashed hands (Mk 7:1-13; Mt 15:1-9). He answered with an angry attack on their practice of *corban*, by which one could avoid the responsibility for supporting an aged parent by offering the support money to the temple. He called them hypocrites and said that they were the blind leading the blind. Jesus was invited to dinner on one occasion by a Pharisee, who rather discourteously observed that Jesus did not wash before dinner. Jesus replied to him, with equal discourtesy, "Oh, you Pharisees! You clean the outside of cup and plate, while inside yourselves you are filled with extortion and wickedness" (Lk 11:37-39; Mt 23:25). Jesus criticized the scribes and Pharisees for placing ritual practices above the law of God:

> You hypocrites, it was a true prophecy Isaiah made of you, writing as he did, This people does me honor with their lips, but its heart is far from me; their worship of me is vain, for the doctrines they teach are the commandments of men. You leave God's commandments on one side, and hold to the tradition of man, the purifying of pitchers and cups, and many other like observances. And he told them, You have quite defeated God's commandment, to establish your own tradition instead. (Mk 7:6-9; Mt 15:7-9)

Jesus opposed the dietary restrictions of the Jewish law. He certainly knew the second chapter of Genesis, where "the Lord God commanded the man, 'You may freely eat of every tree of the garden; but of the tree of the knowledge of good and evil you shall not eat, for in the day that you eat of it you shall die'" (Gen 2:16-17).   But Jesus preached that "what goes into the mouth does not make a man unclean; it is what comes out of the mouth which makes him unclean"

(Mt 15:10-20; Mk 7:14-23). As the author of Mark commented, "Thus he pronounced all foods clean" (Mk 7:19).

Jesus opposed the petty rules of Jewish law. He denounced the religious leaders generally for the multitude of little rules and ritual observances which they taught and enforced, all in the name of Jewish law and tradition:

> Woe to you, scribes and Pharisees, hypocrites! For you tithe mint, dill, and cummin, and have neglected the weightier matters of the law: justice and mercy and faith! It is these you ought to have practiced, without neglecting the others. You blind guides! You strain out a gnat but swallow a camel! (Mt 23:23-24; Lk 11:42)

Paul expressed his understanding of what Jesus had said and done about the Law in Romans: "Now we are discharged from the law, dead to that which held us captive, so that we are servants not under the old written code but in the new life of the Spirit" (Rom 7:6).

The Jews had many rules of shunning, of avoiding contact with people they regarded as unclean or unworthy: tax collectors, prostitutes, adulterers, cripples, blind people, Samaritans, and Gentiles. Remember the parable of the Good Samaritan. Jesus made a point of associating with all of the "unclean," and he and his disciples were often criticized for this. Peter had to learn the lesson all over again when he was called to visit a Roman centurion in Chapter 10 of Acts. Peter said when he first met Cornelius, "You yourselves know that it is unlawful for a Jew to associate with or to visit a Gentile; but God has shown me that I should not call anyone profane or unclean" (Acts 10:28). With this statement, Peter showed that he was finally beginning to understand the commandment of non-judging and was finally free of the Law.

Jesus attacked the central practice of sacrifice. The Pharisees had criticized Jesus to his disciples, saying, "Why does your teacher eat with tax collectors and sinners?" Jesus answered, "Go and learn the meaning of the words: 'I desire mercy, not sacrifice.' For I have come to call not the righteous but sinners" (Mt 9:10-13). He said it again, defending his disciples for picking grain on the Sabbath: "But if you had known what this means, 'I desire mercy and not sacrifice,' you would not have condemned the guiltless" (Mt 12:7). In answer to questions from a scribe, Jesus recited the two great commandments:

Then the scribe said to him, "You are right, Teacher; you have truly said that 'he is one, and besides him there is no other'; and 'to love him with all the heart, and with all the understanding, and with all the strength,' and 'to love one's neighbor as oneself,' – *this is much more important than all whole burnt offerings and sacrifices.*" When Jesus saw that he answered wisely, he said to him, "You are not far from the kingdom of God." (Mk 12:28-34)

Jesus drove out of the Temple in Jerusalem those who were buying and selling sacrificial victims, cattle, sheep, and doves, and the money-changers, thus interrupting the sacrifices in the Temple, only temporarily, but symbolically as well (Jn 2:13-16; Mt 21:12-13; Mk 11:15-17; Lk 19:45-46).

Jesus opposed any public or ostentatious practice of one's religion. In the Sermon on the Mount, he said,

Beware of practicing your piety before others in order to be seen by them; for then you have no reward from your Father in heaven. So whenever you give alms, do not sound a trumpet before you, as the hypocrites do in the synagogues and in the streets, so that they may be praised by others. Truly I tell you, they have received their reward. But when you give alms, do not let your left hand know what your right hand is doing, so that your alms may be done in secret; and your Father who sees in secret will reward you. And whenever you pray, do not be like the hypocrites; for they love to stand and pray in the synagogues and at the street corners, so that they may be seen by others. Truly I tell you, they have received their reward. . . . And whenever you fast, do not look dismal, like the hypocrites, for they disfigure their faces so as to show others that they are fasting. Truly I tell you, they have received their reward. (Mt 6:1-5, 16)

Observance of holy days, holy places, ritual cleanness, ritual dietary restrictions, shunning the unclean, and public prayer were characteristic not simply of Jewish practices but of the practices of all priests of all sacrificial religions. The real object of Jesus's criticisms, and his wholesale rejection of these practices, wasn't the particular ritual laws of the Jews but the religious practices of the culture of sacrifice generally. Thus these criticisms are part of the campaign of Jesus to overturn the foundations of the culture of sacrifice, against which his five commandments are the central thrust.

Jesus prescribed and defined a new and different kind of religion, one without holy days, holy places, rules, rituals, rites of purity, pre-scribed observances and prohibitions, rules of shunning, ostentatious public prayers, or sacrifices. The world had never heard of such a religion. This may explain why all the practices Jesus rejected have eventually found their way back into traditional Christianity.

Replacing the Symbols of Sacrifice.

Jesus prescribed what was to replace the symbols, rules, and prac-tices of the sacrificial culture:

First, he prescribed private and persistent prayer. Jesus repeatedly taught that his followers should pray insistently to the Father: "Ask, and it will be given to you; search, and you will find; knock, and the door will be opened for you" (Mt 7:7). "Whatever you ask for in prayer with faith, you will receive" (Mt 21:22). "Very truly, I tell you, if you ask anything of the Father in my name, he will give it to you" (Jn 16:23).

Jesus showed his command of human psychology when he taught the virtue of persistence in prayer. Because he knew men and women would get discouraged with repeated praying, he urged his followers to persist in prayer even to the point of being a nuisance, like the man who tried to borrow bread from his friend at midnight (Lk 11:5-8), or the widow who kept pestering the unjust judge (Lk 18:1-8). (I don't think he meant that the Father needed pestering; I think he meant that persistence in prayer would be good for us.)

Prayer, Jesus said, is to be a private devotion, not a public and ritual activity:

> But whenever you pray, go into your room and shut the door and pray to your Father who is in secret; and your Father who sees in secret will reward you. (Mt 6:6)

> But when you fast, put oil on your head and wash your face, so that your fasting may be seen not by others but by your Father who is in secret; and your Father who sees in secret will reward you. (Mt 6:17-18)

Jesus taught that prayer, as well as the practice of his five com-mandments, was a matter of a change of mind and of habitual disposition, not a matter of external observances and practices. He taught a grown-up religion to people not ready to leave their immature rituals. When he counseled prayer in secret, I think he intended not rote prayers, but regular and frequent reflective analysis, self-examination, and meditation, as the necessary means to make progress in understanding and observing the five commandments. As he said,

> When you are praying, do not heap up empty phrases as the Gentiles do; for they think that they will be heard because of their many words. Do not be like them, for your Father knows what you need before you ask him. (Mt 6:7-8)

Regular prayerful contemplation of the five commandments of Jesus is a powerful and probably indispensable means of seeing how they may be applied in our personal lives and to the institutions of society. I give examples of the results of such contemplation in Chapters 7 and 8.

Second, Jesus replaced all the symbols of the culture of sacrifice with himself as symbol, sole mentor and leader, and exemplar. This replacement can be seen most clearly in the case of the temple. When Jesus was arguing with the Pharisees about gathering grain on the Sabbath, he said, "Have you not read in the law that on the Sabbath the priests in the temple break the Sabbath and yet are guiltless? I tell you, something greater than the temple is here" (Mt 12:5-6). In the Gospel of John, after the cleansing of the temple,

> The Jews then said to him, "What sign can you show us for doing this?" Jesus answered them, "Destroy this temple, and in three days I will raise it up." The Jews then said, "This temple has been under construction for forty-six years, and will you raise it up in three days?" But he was speaking of the temple of his body. (Jn 2:18-21)

Matthew refers to this saying in his account of the trial of Jesus before the leaders of the Jews:

> At last two came forward and said, "This fellow said, 'I am able to destroy the temple of God and to build it in three days.'" (Mt 26:60-61; *see also* Mt 27:39-40)

Jesus often spoke about his central role in the religious movement he had begun. He claimed to be God's exclusive representative on earth, and the exclusive teacher of truth about God:

> All things have been handed over to me by my Father; and no one knows the Son except the Father, and no one knows the

Father except the Son and anyone to whom the Son chooses to reveal him. (Mt 11:27; Lk 10:22)

Jesus accepted the title of Messiah, or "anointed one" (in Greek, the *Christos*, hence Jesus Christ), the one who is to come as king to liberate Israel and restore her people as the true chosen people of God:

Jesus went on with his disciples to the villages of Caesarea Philippi; and on the way he asked his disciples, "Who do people say that I am?" And they answered him, "John the Baptist; and others, Elijah; and still others, one of the prophets." He asked them, "But who do you say that I am?" Peter answered him, "You are the Messiah." And he sternly ordered them not to tell anyone about him. (Mk 8:27-30; Mt 16:13-17; Lk 9:18-20)

At his trial before the high priest of the Jews, the night before his execution, he formally accepted the title, quoting Daniel the prophet:

Again the high priest asked him, "Are you the Messiah, the Son of the Blessed One?" Jesus said, "I am; and 'you will see the Son of Man seated at the right hand of the Power,' and 'coming with the clouds of heaven.'" (Mk 14:61-62; Mt 26:63-64; Lk 22:67-69)

Jesus asserted that he would have the role of judge at the Last Judgment, saying, "For the Son of Man is to come with his angels in the glory of his Father, and then he will repay everyone for what has been done" (Mt 16:27). And he said,

When the Son of Man comes in his glory, and all the angels with him, then he will sit on the throne of his glory. All the nations will be gathered before him, and he will separate people one from another as a shepherd separates the sheep from the goats, and he will put the sheep at his right hand and the goats at the left. (Mt 25:31-33)

Jesus identified himself with his message. He acted out the virtues of non-judging, forgiveness, nonviolence, disregard of hierarchy, and poverty. He didn't expect his disciples to act better than he did, nor to go where he had not gone. "A disciple is not above the teacher, nor a servant above the master; it is enough for the disciple to be like the teacher, and the servant like the master" (Mt 10:24-25; Lk 6:40; Jn 13:16). He was quite clear about who was the teacher and who was the disciple: "You are not to be called rabbi, for you have one teacher, and you are all students" (Mt 23:8).   Particularly in the Gospel of John, Jesus used vivid metaphors to illustrate his identification of his person with his message: "I am the bread of life. . . . Whoever eats of this bread will live forever" (Jn 6:48, 51).   "I am the light of the world. Whoever follows me will never walk in darkness but will have the light of life" (Jn 8:12).   "I am the resurrection and the life.   Those who believe in me, even though they die, will live" (Jn 11:25).

Jesus claimed that the identification of his message and his person is unique and perfect:

> I am the way, and the truth, and the life.   No one comes to the Father except through me. (Jn 14:6)

> As a branch cannot bear fruit all by itself, but must remain part of the vine, neither can you unless you remain in me.   I am the vine, you are the branches.   Whoever remains in me, with me in him, bears fruit in plenty; for cut off from me you can do nothing. (Jn 15:4-5)

> Come to me, all you who are weary and are carrying heavy burdens, and I will give you rest.   Take my yoke upon you, and learn from me; for I am gentle and humble in heart, and you will find rest for your souls.   For my yoke is easy and my burden is light. (Mt 11:28-30)

Third and finally, Jesus rejected the idea of a God who is cruel and wrathful enough to demand sacrifices, or so inconstant or mercurial as to be moved magically to reward or punish a person based on the gifts or sacrifices he or she has given.   Jesus taught that God is neither the wrathful, vengeful, tribal God of the Hebrew Scriptures nor a capricious, indifferent pagan god.   Nor is God the remote, abstract God of philosophers.   God is, above all, a Father, said Jesus, with all the paternal virtues of a good human father, but in perfection.   Before Jesus taught, it was unknown to speak of God as a Father, but Jesus always did so, using an affectionate and intimate term, Abba, Father. Jesus taught that God takes care of those who trust in him:

> Therefore do not worry, saying "What will we eat?" or "What will we drink?" or "What will we wear?"   For . . . your heavenly Father knows that you need all these things.   But strive first for the kingdom of God and his righteousness, and all these things will be given to you as well. (Mt 6:31-32; Lk 12:29-31)

> Are not five sparrows sold for two pennies? Yet not one of them is forgotten in God's sight. But even the hairs of your head are all counted. Do not be afraid; you are of more value than many sparrows. (Lk 12:6-7; Mt 10:29-31)

God forgives those who repent, he asserted:

> There will be more joy in heaven over one sinner who repents than over ninety-nine righteous persons who need no repentance. (Lk 15:7; Mt 18:13)

Like the father of the Prodigal Son (Lk 15:11-32), God is always ready to forgive his children, Jesus taught, and does so freely and gratuitously, out of his fatherly benevolence.

Jesus taught that God's justice and mercy are not always found in this life. The evil that befalls some of us isn't a punishment for sin. The good life that some others of us enjoy isn't a reward for virtuous conduct. Jesus taught that the Father "makes his sun rise on the evil and on the good, and sends his rain to fall on the honest and dishonest alike" (Mt 5:45). This sounds simple, and it seems obvious to us; but it is neither. It's a profound observation about the realities of human life on earth. In the parable of the wheat and the weeds, set forth above, the farmer whose enemy sowed weeds in his wheat field does not let his field hands weed the fields, lest in gathering the weeds they would uproot the wheat. "Let both of them grow together until the harvest; and at harvest time I will tell the reapers, collect the weeds first and bind them in bundles to be burned, but gather the wheat into my barn" (Mt 13:30). Jesus taught that God will do the same.

The disciples of Jesus had a hard time understanding that misfortune in life isn't a punishment for sin. When they saw a man who had been born blind, they asked Jesus, "'Rabbi, who sinned, this man or his parents, that he was born blind?' Jesus answered, 'Neither this man nor his parents sinned; he was born blind so that God's works might be revealed in him'" (Jn 9:1-3).

Jesus taught that God is love: "Those who love me will keep my word, and my Father will love them, and we will come to them and make our abode with them" (Jn 14:23). "For God so loved the world that he gave his only begotten Son, that whosoever believes in him should not perish, but have everlasting life" (Jn 3:16).

THE KINGDOM AND THE END OF SACRIFICE

Jesus many times promised that God would be with his followers in this life, to provide guidance and help when needed. Here is some of what he said:

> When they bring you before the synagogues, the rulers, and the authorities, do not worry about how you are to defend yourselves or what you are to say, for the Holy Spirit will teach you at that very hour what you ought to say. (Lk 12:11-12; Mt 10:19-20; Mk 13:11)

> And I will ask the Father, and he will give you another Advocate, to be with you forever. This is the Spirit of truth. (Jn 14:16-17)

> Those who love me will keep my word, and my Father will love them, and we will come to them and make our abode with them. (Jn 14:23)

> And remember, I am with you always, to the end of the age. (Mt 28:20)

Note that Jesus observed no consistency in what he called this continuing presence of God. Sometimes he called it the presence of the Holy Spirit. Other times he spoke of the presence of the Father, or of his own continuing presence.

We turn now to the death and resurrection of Jesus.

VI

The Death and Resurrection of Jesus

"But take courage; I have conquered the world!" (Jn 16:33)

As we've seen, Jesus's teaching of his five commandments and his teachings against the sacrifice and its associated rules and practices are the two parts of his systematic campaign against the anti-social genetically based behaviors and the culture of sacrifice which had absorbed and embedded these behaviors in human social, cultural, and political institutions. By his death and resurrection, Jesus completed these teachings, gave us potent and profound symbols of the message he had taught, lived, and died for, and assured that his campaign and his message would survive.

The story of the passion and death of Jesus is told in all four Gospels. In all essentials and in most of the details, the stories are in full agreement. There are minor differences, consistent with the fact that the four Gospels record five different oral traditions developed over the first two generations of Christians. For example, in Luke's narrative, and only there, when Jesus arrived at Pilate's door, Pilate sent him to Herod Antipas, who ruled in Galilee, because Jesus was a Galilean. After questioning Jesus to no avail, Herod sent him back to Pilate (Lk 23:6-12). In Matthew's narrative only, Pilate's wife sent him a message to have nothing to do with Jesus, and Pilate washed his hands before the mob (Mt 27:19, 24). In Mark, Jesus tells Peter that before the cock crows twice, Peter will deny him three times (Mk 14:30); in the other Gospels, the same story is told with only one cock crow (Mt 26:34; Lk 22:34; Jn 13:38). Apart from a number of minor variances of this kind, the passion stories are substantially consistent with each other.

So the facts of the arrest, trials, torture, and execution of Jesus are well documented and relatively clear. What's less clear is why did it happen? What did the various parties intend to accomplish, and what does it mean?

We begin by looking at the motives of the people who brought Jesus to his death. Israel of the time of Jesus was a small theocratic state located at a crossroads of the Middle East. For centuries it had been dominated by one or another regional empire: the Assyrians, the Babylonians, the Persians, and at the time of Jesus the Roman Empire. Israel maintained its identity and a measure of self-rule only by the most rigorous and stubborn adherence to its separate and superior status as God's chosen people, and, as we saw in Chapter 5, to the innumerable prohibitions and rules of conduct which made up its Law, regulating external actions in minute detail. There was a professional class of scholars of the Law, the scribes and Pharisees, who told everyone else what they could or could not do, and a hereditary professional class of priests, who controlled all the sacrificial services.

It's evident throughout the Gospels that Jesus and his healing and teaching ministry threatened the priests, the scribes, and the Pharisees. They reasonably concluded that his teaching could destroy Israel in either or both of two ways. One risk was that he'd succeed in his efforts to undermine the Sabbath prohibitions, the cleanness rules, the dietary proscriptions, and so forth, while preaching love of enemies, non-judging, and the like, so that the Jews would become just like their neighbors and would lose the separateness and ethnic solidarity which kept them together as the chosen people. Another risk was that he'd use his charismatic power over his disciples and followers to stir up a revolt against the Romans, who would defeat and then disperse the Jews. (A few self-proclaimed "Messiahs" among the Jews did do this at various times in the first century A.D., and finally the Romans did defeat and disperse the Jews.)

The chief priests and Pharisees had said to each other about Jesus, "If we let him go on like this, everyone will believe in him, and the Romans will come and destroy both our holy place and our nation" (Jn 11:48). Either way, Israel would be destroyed, and the priests, scribes, and Pharisees would all lose their jobs and their lives' work. It was a real crisis for Israel. Jesus had to be "terminated with prejudice." The high priest Caiaphas, talking to the Jewish leaders, put his finger on it: "You know nothing at all! You do not understand that it is better for you to have one man die for the people, than to have the whole nation destroyed" (Jn 11:49-50).

So the leaders of the Jews put together a plan to have Jesus executed, and they carried it out. They bribed one of his disciples, Judas Iscariot, to arrange a private place, the garden of Gethsemani, where the temple guards could capture him; they couldn't do it in public for fear of the people (Mt 26:5; Mk 14:2; Lk 22:6). There they sent the temple guards to arrest Jesus. All the disciples deserted him and fled (Mt 26:56; Mk 14:50). They held a midnight kangaroo court trial, where Jesus was mocked and slapped around. Early the next morning, they brought him to Pilate, along with a mob they had organized. Pilate tried to avoid their demand for the death of Jesus by offering to release to the mob either Jesus or Barabbas, an insurgent and murderer. The leaders of the Jews led the mob to call for the release of Barabbas and for the crucifixion of Jesus. Pilate, afraid of the potential for riot, condemned Jesus to death and handed him over for crucifixion. His soldiers scourged Jesus, crowned him with thorns, mocked him, led him out to the hill of Golgotha, and crucified him.

Was this a sacrifice? In the sense of a ritual blood sacrifice, certainly not. Was it a scapegoat sacrifice, a lynching, of the kind described near the end of Chapter 3? It certainly was. All the elements are there: a social crisis, the angry mob, the identification of an innocent victim, transference of blame to the victim, desertion of the victim by his supporters or allies, and accusations of fantastic crimes:

> Now the chief priests and the whole council were looking for false testimony against Jesus so that they might put him to death, but they found none, though many false witnesses came forward. At last two came forward and said, "This fellow said, 'I am able to destroy the temple of God and to build it in three days.'" (Mt 26:59-61; Mk 14:55-59)

Even the random choice of victim is present, as the mob is asked to choose between Jesus and Barabbas.

As a scapegoat lynching, it should have worked. The followers of Jesus who deserted him should have dispersed, and the city should have been rid of this troublesome sect. But it didn't work out that way.

Let's turn to Jesus. How did he understand the danger of the situation with the leaders of the Jews, and what did he have in mind? To begin with, Jesus was a realistic man. He knew that he had been attacking most of the traditions, laws, and religious practices of Israel. He knew that the priests, scribes, and Pharisees were exceedingly angry and hostile, and that many of them had been talking among themselves about putting him to death. He didn't need to be a prophet to see that unless he ceased his preaching and healing activities, or got out of the country, neither of which he had any intention of doing, he would eventually be killed by the Jews, the Romans, or both together.

Jesus had faced death threats earlier in his ministry and had somehow escaped. Luke documents his preaching in Nazareth, which so inflamed the congregation that

> when they heard this, all in the synagogue were filled with rage. They got up, drove him out of the town, and led him to the brow of the hill on which their town was built, so that they might hurl him off the cliff. But he passed through the midst of them and went on his way. (Lk 4:28-30)

Two things are interesting in this story. First, forcing a victim over the edge of a cliff is one of the classic forms of execution of a sacrificial victim; another is stoning (which Jesus would also face). What they have in common is that all are involved in the killing; no one can tell who in the pressing mob forced the victim to take the final fatal step, or who threw the killing stone. Second, how does the victim "pass through the midst" of an angry lynch mob? Luke doesn't tell us.

The author of John documents two such occasions. At the end of the heated debate in John Chapter 8,

> Jesus said to them, "Very truly, I tell you, before Abraham was, I am." So they picked up stones to throw at him, but Jesus hid himself and went out of the temple. (Jn 8:58-59)

And at the end of the Good Shepherd teaching in John Chapter 10,

> The Jews took up stones again to stone him. Jesus replied, "I have shown you many good works from the Father. For which of these are you going to stone me?" The Jews answered, "It is not for a good work that we are going to stone you, but for blasphemy, because you, though only a human being, are making yourself God." . . . Then they tried to arrest him again, but he escaped from their hands. (Jn 10:31-33, 39)

When Jesus was arrested in the garden of Gethsemani, he told his disciples not to fight for his freedom, saying,

> Do you think that I cannot appeal to my Father, and he will at once send me more than twelve legions of angels? But how then would the scriptures be fulfilled, which say it must happen in this way? (Mt 26:53-54)

It seems that Jesus could've avoided death indefinitely, but that on this occasion he chose not to. He was in this sense in control of the time, place, and manner of his own death. As he said,

> I lay down my life in order to take it up again. No one takes it from me, but I lay it down of my own accord. I have power to lay it down, and I have power to take it up again. (Jn 10:17-18)

Why at this time didn't Jesus avoid the death he so clearly foresaw? Since he went willingly to his own clearly foreseen death, the question is why did he do so, and what did he intend his death to accomplish?

In my view, what Jesus had in mind was his belief that his death would be followed in quick order by his resurrection from the dead, not to his former life, as was the case with the daughter of Jairus, the son of the widow of Naim, and Lazarus, all of whom he had raised from the dead, but to a new life, a life after death. As in the case of the miracles of Jesus, many people of our time, particularly educated people, have an *a priori* conviction that the resurrection from the dead could not have occurred. Now if the resurrection couldn't have happened, it makes little sense to say that Jesus foresaw it. If the resurrection couldn't and thus didn't happen, we'd have to explain how the early Christians first agreed among themselves that Jesus did rise from the dead, then went to the trouble to have all the gospel writers insert into their narratives bogus sayings of Jesus predicting his death and resurrection and extended narratives of the empty tomb and of his appearances after his resurrection, and finally went forth to convert Jews and Gentiles as if they all believed it. That would be a conspiracy worthy of Robert Ludlum or Dan Brown, and it strains my credulity. Bearing in mind this problem, I'll set forth the evidence that Jesus did foresee not only his death, but also his resurrection, and later in the chapter I'll describe the evidence for the resurrection itself.

According to the Gospels, Jesus repeatedly told his disciples that he would be executed and then would rise again on the third day, four times in direct language and two additional times in metaphor or analogy:

> Then he began to teach them that the Son of Man must undergo great suffering, and be rejected by the elders, the chief priests, and the scribes, and after three days rise again. He said all this quite openly. And Peter took him aside and

began to rebuke him. But turning and looking at his disciples, he rebuked Peter and said, "Get behind me, Satan! For you are setting your mind not on divine things but on human things." (Mk 8:31-33; Mt 16:21-23; Lk 9:21-22)

He was teaching his disciples, saying to them, "The Son of Man is to be betrayed into human hands, and they will kill him, and three days after being killed, he will rise again." But they did not understand what he was saying and were afraid to ask him. (Mk 9:31-32; Mt 17:22-23; Lk 9:43-45)

They were on the road, going up to Jerusalem, and Jesus was walking ahead of them; they were amazed, and those who followed were afraid. He took the twelve aside again and began to tell them what was going to happen to him, saying, "See, we are going up to Jerusalem, and the Son of Man will be handed over to the chief priests and the scribes, and they will condemn him to death; then they will hand him over to the Gentiles; they will mock him, and spit on him, and flog him, and kill him; and after three days he will rise again." (Mk 10:32-34; Mt 20:17-19; Lk 18:31-33)

Then some of the scribes and Pharisees said to him, "Teacher, we wish to see a sign from you." But he answered them, "An evil and adulterous generation asks for a sign, but no sign will be given except the sign of the prophet Jonah. For just as Jonah was three days and three nights in the belly of the sea monster, so for three days and three nights the Son of Man will be in the heart of the earth." (Mt 12:38-40; Lk 11:29-30)

The Jews then said to him, "What sign can you show us for doing this?" Jesus answered them, "Destroy this temple, and in three days I will raise it up." The Jews then said, "This temple has been under construction for forty-six years, and will you raise it up in three days?" But he was speaking about the temple of his body. (Jn 2:19-21; *see also* Mt 26:61; Mt 27:40; Mk 14:58)

Then Jesus said to them, "You will all become deserters because of me this night; for it is written, 'I will strike the shepherd, and the sheep of the flock will be scattered.' But after I am raised up, I will go before you to Galilee." (Mt 26:31-32; Mk 14:27-28)

Before discussing these prophecies as a group, let's look in particular at the sign of Jonah prediction. The story of Jonah and the whale (or sea monster) is familiar, and Jesus makes express reference to it. What's less well known is how Jonah got into the whale in the first place. According to the story, God had told Jonah to preach repentance in Nineveh, but Jonah didn't want to go there and took a ship in the opposite direction. God sent a storm which threatened to destroy the ship. The terrified sailors drew lots to find out who was at fault, and the lot fell on Jonah. After some dialogue, the sailors threw Jonah into the sea (Jonah 1:1-15). So Jonah was a classic scapegoat, a victim chosen at random by the mob and thrown to death. The sign of Jonah is the sign of a scapegoat sacrifice as well as a sign of someone who returned from the dead.

Looking at the death-and-resurrection prophecies as a group, we see that they are found in four of the five Gospel sources or traditions (Mark, Q, Matthew, and John) and are expressed both directly and in metaphor and parable. They go back to the earliest New Testament tradition. Thus it's highly probable that they are Jesus's own sayings and that Jesus did believe that he would be put to death and would rise again.

One factor which I personally find persuasive on this issue is the attitude toward his imminent death which Jesus maintained throughout. Jesus believed that he would rise on the third day with the same certainty and clarity of vision with which he knew that he would be put to death: no hesitation, no fear, no doubt. Jesus never looked at his own approaching death the way the rest of us look toward our own deaths, with trepidation and the fear that this may be the permanent end of our consciousness and our personal existence. Jesus seems always to have seen his death as one with the resurrection which would very shortly follow, as his statements quoted above indicate. Thus it's always not his death but his "death-and-resurrection" as one single event which he had in mind. At the Last Supper, he gave us a parable to help us understand this:

> When a woman is in labor, she has pain, because her hour has come. But when her child is born, she no longer remembers the anguish because of the joy of having brought a human being into the world. (Jn 16:21)

Jesus no more thought about his death apart from his resurrection than a woman thinks about her labor without thinking of the child who is being born. Thus it doesn't make sense to me to study the attitude of

Jesus with respect to his death without considering his foreknowledge of his own resurrection.

With two exceptions, the passion narratives show Jesus as calm, fearless, and unyielding. Normal human fear of death seems not to have touched him. He was more concerned with the sufferings of others than with his own suffering, even on the way of the cross. On the road to Calvary,

> A great number of the people followed him, and among them were women who were beating their breasts and wailing for him. But Jesus turned to them and said, "Daughters of Jerusalem, do not weep for me, but weep for yourselves and for your children. For the days are surely coming when they will say, 'Blessed are the barren, and the wombs that never bore, and the breasts that never nursed.' Then they will begin to say to the mountains, 'Fall on us'; and to the hill, 'Cover us.' For if they do this when the wood is green, what will happen when it is dry?" (Lk 23:27-31)

Jesus wasn't taking their future sufferings on himself; they would certainly suffer; he was simply more concerned about their future sufferings than about his own present ones.

In his extended Last Supper discourse, Jesus spoke of his own joy: "If you loved me, you would rejoice that I am going to the Father, because the Father is greater than I" (Jn 14:28). "I have said these things to you so that my joy may be in you, and that your joy may be complete" (Jn 15:11). "But now I am coming to you [the Father], and I speak these things in the world so that they may have my joy made complete in themselves" (Jn 17:13). These words couldn't have been spoken by a man facing death within the next several hours. They're the words of a man looking forward to his death-and-resurrection.

One exception is the agony in the garden, where Jesus is said to have prayed that he might avoid the passion and death (Mt 26:36-46; Mk 14:32-42; Lk 22:39-46). I have two problems with the agony in the garden story. First, the story shows an irresolution and self-doubt in Jesus which seems out of character with everything else he's reported to have said and did. Perhaps he thought it a useful way to prepare for the physical ordeal of the passion by letting his mind block the resurrection and concentrate on the physical pain he would have to endure? This seems unlikely, but I don't know how else to interpret his words. Second, and more telling, the agony in the garden is one of the very few stories of Jesus which record his words at a time when, according to the story itself, he was alone and no one could have heard his words. (The twelve had been left behind, and the three were asleep. Who heard the prayers of Jesus?) So I'm inclined to believe that the story of the agony in the garden is an invention of the early Church.

The second exception is the cry of Jesus from the cross, "'*Eli, Eli, lema sabachthani?*' that is, 'My God, my God, why have you forsaken me?'" (Mt 27:46; Mk 15:34). This is often taken as a cry of despair. But what Jesus was doing was reciting the first line of Psalm 22, and as a devout Jew, Jesus would have had in mind the entire Psalm. Psalm 22 both foreshadows in some detail what Jesus was undergoing at the time and is a prayer of faith, courage, and great hope. Later in the Psalm, the psalmist says, "For he did not despise nor abhor the affliction of the afflicted; he did not hide his face from me, but heard when I cried to him" (Ps 22:24). The entire second half of Psalm 22 is a hymn of hope and confidence in God. By referring to this Psalm, Jesus was able to make a complex and prayerful literary allusion to his own situation and to his abiding trust in God when he was on the point of death. I think this supports my assertion that Jesus approached his own death with calm and with confidence in his Father.

Jesus had an agenda, a program, a plan, throughout his public life. He didn't need to be a prophet to know that he was in mortal danger from the leaders of the Jews. He had avoided death several times before. Yet on his last trip to Jerusalem to celebrate the Passover, he took no steps to avoid danger and seemed to accept willingly his capture by the temple guards. What did he have in mind? Well, we don't know for sure, because he didn't say.

But we do know some of the effects of his death, and some of the effects of his resurrection. In several ways, some physical, some exemplary, and some symbolic, these effects completed his work and concluded his mission. Let's examine six of the effects of the death-and-resurrection of Jesus in this light.

1.   *Inversion of Values.* Jesus had preached an overturning and inversion of the values of Israel and of the pagan world. His five commandments instructed his followers to love and forgive their enemies, not to judge or hate them, and not to take revenge. They were to be humble servants, and to detach themselves from posses-sions. All of these attitudes were exactly the opposite of what the

world believed. Jesus had attacked all the religious values of his society: rules of ritual purity, ritual cleanness, dietary restrictions, rules of shunning, holy times, holy places, the sacrifice, and the religious hierarchy itself. Inversion of values runs through all his teachings. He generalized this inversion, saying repeatedly that "the last will be first, and the first will be last," and that "all who exalt themselves will be humbled, and all who humble themselves will be exalted." His death-and-resurrection turned out to be the one final and focal demonstration and symbol of this inversion of the values of the world. The disgraced, convicted, and executed criminal would become the teacher and leader of a great religious movement, and he would be exalted to divinity by his followers. The cross, the death instrument of ignominy, is the symbol of Christianity because it's the symbol of this complete inversion of values.

2.   *Fidelity to Death.*   Jesus had frequently warned his disciples that they would be persecuted and killed for fidelity to his name and his teachings. "Then they will hand you over to be tortured and will put you to death, and you will be hated by all nations because of my name" (Mt 24:9). "Indeed, an hour is coming when those who kill you will think that by doing so they are offering worship to God" (Jn 16:2). Jesus had called his disciples to stay true to his ideals even in the face of death, and he never asked his disciples to do what he was unwilling or unable to do. In his death, whether he rose again or not, Jesus showed his disciples that he also had gone through torture and death rather than betray the principles and practices of the kingdom and of his mission.

3.   *Confirmation of God's Approval.*   Jesus had worked wonders and great signs so that men and women would believe that his words and his deeds were approved by the God of Israel. There was one sign, however, which would tower above all the others, as the central and focal sign of God's confirmation of the unique truth of his teaching and his mission. His death-and-resurrection would be the preeminent symbol and confirmation of the victory of God in him.

4.   *Resurrection of the Body.*   Jesus had one major teaching which could be, but had not yet been, demonstrated in his own life: that humans will pass through death and live again in the body. Death isn't the end; it's simply a change. The Latin Requiem Mass says, in its Preface, *"Tuis enim fidelibus, Domine, vita mutatur, non tollitur."* ("To your

faithful, Lord, life is changed, not taken away.") This is the final lesson, the final victory. As Paul tells us, "The last enemy to be destroyed is death" (1 Cor 15:26). This great promise and this revelation were confirmed and demonstrated by the death-and-resurrection of Jesus.

5.   *Awakening the Disciples.* The disciples of Jesus clearly needed some galvanizing, life-changing experience so that they could and would act independently in his absence. They had certainly shown little sign during his lifetime of the courage or the understanding needed for their mission. We may assume that Jesus, an astute observer of men, had chosen his disciples carefully and well, but for much of his public life it didn't appear so. Yet he remained confident in them, as his last discourse to them shows. They had followed him, in spite of difficulties, for the duration of his ministry. They had put their hopes in him, but upon his capture in Gethsemani, they had all deserted him and fled. The psychological impact upon them of his ignominious execution was, as we can well imagine, devastating. Their lives and hopes were in ruins.

Then a few days after the death and burial of Jesus, something life-changing happened to them. They described it as seeing the risen Jesus. They were astonished and exalted. They had lost everything, and now to their amazement they found that they had won. It was all true. They then set about with great boldness and courage to preach the message of the risen Jesus. See the first several chapters of the Acts of the Apostles. The extraordinary history of the first generation of the Christian church shows the results of this great awakening.

6.   *Revealing and Negating the Sacrifice.* The sixth effect of the death-and-resurrection of Jesus is more complicated and subtle than the first five. It shows Jesus as a kind of judo master, as the power and lethal force directed toward him by the Jews and the Romans was somehow turned against them to defeat their purposes and to reinforce the central thrust of his teachings. The effect was to destroy the institution of sacrifice by exposing to view the primal lie upon which it is based.

As we saw in Chapter 3, the human sacrifice of ancient and prehistoric times was always at bottom a murder, a lynching. It was always accompanied by a lie, the primal lie, that the victim is to blame for the murder. The myth which preserves the story of the sacrifice conceals the murder and hides the transfer of guilt from the sacrificers to the victim. The scapegoating sacrifice works the same way and is based on the same lie: the victim is to blame. Ritual human sacrifice had embedded itself in, and had remained at the foundation of, human civilizations until the time of Jesus. The scapegoating sacrifice remains embedded in our civilizations today.

The sacrifice persists because both the murder and the lie are hidden. By his death, Jesus ended the sacrifice and substituted another way to obtain human peace and unity. He knew that he'd be the designated victim of a scapegoating sacrifice, as his reference to the sign of Jonah shows. He personally believed that this sacrifice would fail, as the sign of Jonah also shows. The victim died, but he didn't stay dead. The followers of the victim fled, but then reunited with new-found courage, vigor, and audacity, because they all believed that Jesus had risen from the dead. They started a movement which grew so rapidly that in two generations there were Christian communities in all the major cities of the Mediterranean world.

In the same period of time, they succeeded in producing four different but consistent narrative descriptions of the arrest, trial, and execution of Jesus, *all from the victim's point of view*. All of the elements of the classic scapegoating sacrifice or lynching are in place; but in the narratives of the passion and death of Jesus they are *visibly* in place. The victim is clearly seen to be innocent; the charges against him are obviously outlandish or spurious; the mob which gathers to condemn Jesus is seen as manipulated by a small coterie of enemies of Jesus; and the mock legal process is revealed as a criminal conspiracy. From this time forward, now that the innocence of the victim can be clearly seen, the psychological transfer of blame and guilt from the sacrificers to the victim can no longer take place; and without that transfer the sacrifice can no longer work.

It's from the crucifixion of Jesus that the Western world has learned to see persecution and scapegoating from the viewpoint of the victim. That's why ritual human sacrifice is no longer performed in any civilization which has been reached by the Christian message. That's why we're shocked at the Christian persecutions of Jews in the Middle Ages, at the Spanish Inquisition, at the witch hunts and trials of the sixteenth and seventeenth centuries, and at the lynchings of African-Americans in the United States a century ago, and why we don't believe the stories of the persecutors when they blame their victims.

This understanding of the death of Jesus as revealing the hidden elements of the sacrifice, thereby negating their power and influence, wasn't understood in early Christianity. Because people at the time of Jesus still generally believed that human sacrifice was the appropriate way to propitiate an angry deity, and hadn't sufficiently reflected upon what the death of Jesus reveals about sacrifice, much of traditional Christianity has for a long time mistakenly interpreted his death not as an anti-sacrificial revelation but as itself a sacrifice. But the one thing Jesus didn't do in his death-and-resurrection was to offer himself as a human sacrifice for the sins of humanity. He didn't take the sins of humans on himself, because responsibility and guilt for our own sins is something that no human being can transfer to another.

To believe that the death of Jesus was an expiatory blood sacrifice is to repeat the primal lie of our most ancient forebears. It's to transfer sin, blame, and guilt to the victim, and then make the victim a god, a god who asked for the lynching and is pleased by the lynching. It's to tell the story of the death of Jesus again from the point of view of the persecutors, which is exactly the opposite of what the Gospels reveal. It's to reduce the Father in heaven to the status of a wrathful and vengeful pagan god. It implies that what Jesus was doing was changing God's mind about humanity, not our minds about God. It negates everything Jesus stood for, and died for.

The death-and-resurrection of Jesus must be understood in a way which is consistent with his life and teaching. As his teachings attacked the foundations of the culture of sacrifice, the genetically based behaviors, and the sacrifice itself, and proposed an alternative way of living, so his death-and-resurrection completed that teaching. Thus the pagan sacrifice, and all it stood for, was overturned and destroyed in his death-and-resurrection.

These are the principal effects or consequences of the death-and-resurrection of Jesus. Did Jesus have any of these effects in mind as he approached his death? Did he have a conscious purpose and intent to accomplish these effects? If one doesn't believe that the resurrection, or some event which would be the symbolic and practical equivalent of the resurrection, occurred, it would be difficult to conclude that Jesus foresaw his resurrection. It would thus be difficult to see how he could've expected, much less intended, these consequences, with the exception of fidelity to death, which isn't dependent on the resurrection.

Even if one believes in the physical resurrection of Jesus from the dead, as I do, it doesn't follow that Jesus had these effects in mind and consciously intended to cause them to happen. He never told us. My own view, however, is that it makes a great deal of sense to conclude that Jesus very probably had these consequences of his death-and-resurrection in mind and consciously intended to accomplish them, because each of these consequences completes the work that he did during his life in an important and significant way. Each consequence brings a portion of his teachings to a conclusion consistent with all he said and did. Finally, it explains how Jesus was able to approach his death without doubt or fear, with concern for the sufferings of others rather than for his own, and, if the author of John reports correctly, with joy. It explains why Jesus was able, at the Last Supper, to reassure his disciples, saying, "Take courage; I have conquered the world!" (Jn 16:33).

We turn now to the evidence which has persuaded me that Jesus physically rose from the dead.

The first evidence is that of the empty tomb, which all the Gospels describe (Mt 28:1-10; Mk 16:1-8; Lk 24:1-12; Jn 20:1-10). Here is Mark's version:

> When the Sabbath was over, Mary Magdalene, and Mary the mother of James, and Salome bought spices, so that they might go and anoint him. And very early on the first day of the week, when the sun had risen, they went to the tomb. They had been saying to one another, "Who will roll away the stone for us from the entrance to the tomb?" When they looked up, they saw that the stone, which was very large, had already been rolled back. As they entered the tomb, they saw a young man, dressed in a white robe, sitting on the right side; and they were alarmed. But he said to them, "Do not be alarmed; you are looking for Jesus of Nazareth, who was crucified. He has been raised; he is not here. Look, there is the place they laid him. But go, tell his disciples and Peter that he is going ahead of you to Galilee; there you will see him, just as he told you." So they went out and fled from the tomb, for terror and amazement had seized them; and they said nothing to anyone, for they were afraid. (Mk 16:1-8)

The first and most important fact in the history of Christianity is the testimony and preaching of a considerable number of people, all of whom said that they had personally seen the risen Jesus. All the remaining eleven apostles claimed to have seen the risen Jesus. When, after Jesus had left them, they decided to select a twelfth apostle to fill the place of Judas, their criterion was to choose a man who had followed Jesus for his entire public ministry and who had seen the risen Jesus (Acts 1:21-22). All of the sermons recorded in the Acts of the Apostles have the resurrection of Jesus as their central theme. The resurrection was critical to Paul, who said, "If Christ has not been raised, then our proclamation has been in vain and your faith has been in vain" (1 Cor 15:14). Belief in the resurrection preceded belief in the Gospels, because if the resurrection had not been believed there would have been no need for or occasion for the Gospels. No one would have bothered to write them.

The New Testament contains no fewer than twenty references to appearances of the risen Jesus, describing about eleven separate appearances, six of which are reported by two or three authors. Jesus appeared:

1.   to Mary Magdalene (Mk 16:9; Jn 20:14-18);
2.   to Mary Magdalene and the other Mary (Mt 28:9-10);
3.   to two disciples on the road to Emmaus (Mk 16:12; Lk 24:13-32);
4.   to Peter (Lk 24:34; 1 Cor 15:5);
5.   to James (1 Cor 15:7);
6.   to all the disciples except Thomas, the evening of the first day (Lk 24:36-43; Jn 20:19-23; 1 Cor 15:5);
7.   to all the disciples, a week later (Mk 16:14; Jn 20:24-29);
8.   by the sea of Tiberias, to seven disciples (Jn 21:1-23);
9.   to all the disciples on a mountain in Galilee (Mt 28:16-18);
10. to more than five hundred of the brethren, most of whom were still alive twenty-five years later, when St. Paul wrote of it (1 Cor 15:6); and
11. at his ascension, to a large group of disciples (Mk 16:19; Lk 24:50-51; Acts 1:6-11).

It's a substantial body of testimonial evidence. I don't think it's plausible that such a large group of people could have invented the story of the resurrection, formed a conspiracy to spread it, and then maintained that conspiracy for the rest of their lives. Some authors have suggested that the witnesses to the risen Christ were hallucinating, in the emotional grip of a wish to see Jesus again. But if they were hallucinating, why did they hallucinate someone they didn't recognize? Mary Magdalene saw the risen Jesus and at first thought he was the gardener (Jn 20:15). The disciples on the road to Emmaus thought Jesus was a fellow traveler and didn't recognize him until after a long walk and a long conversation (Lk 24:16). And none of the seven disciples who saw Jesus from the boat on the sea of Tiberias knew who he was (Jn 21:4).

The way Jesus appeared is interesting. He didn't appear as a vision, as a spirit, or as a ghost; he appeared as a man in the flesh. He bore the wounds of his death. It wasn't as if he had never been dead; he appeared as one who had been dead and was now fully alive. He could be touched. He could be, and was, mistaken for a gardener or a fellow traveler on the road. On two occasions he joined his disciples in a meal of broiled fish. He was ordinary in these respects, except that he seemed to have gained a facility of appearing and disappearing. When the disciples fishing on the Lake of Tiberias saw him from the boat, and after some time recognized him, they came to the shore. There they found that the risen Jesus had built a charcoal fire and was grilling fish. "Come and have breakfast," he said (Jn 21:12). In a strange way, these words strike me as among the most encouraging and comforting things Jesus ever said. In contrast to the narratives of the incarnation, birth, and early childhood of Jesus, the narratives of his appearances after his resurrection are neither mythic nor poetic, but appear to be direct testimony, simply and humanly documented.

The resurrection of Jesus is the single most important miracle of the life of Jesus. There are some learned and committed Christians who have difficulty believing this miracle, and many of us have difficulty some of the time believing that it actually took place. Science and the experience of mankind certainly show that the resurrection of a person from the dead is (as far as we know) exceedingly rare and thus highly unlikely, but they can't show that it is impossible. Whether we admit that it took place on this one occasion depends on the evidence. In the law the best evidence is the testimony of an eyewitness. Other evidence is circumstantial, and it's frequently regarded as less reliable, as when we say, "Oh, the evidence against him was purely circumstantial" or "He was convicted on circumstantial evidence." The evidence described above, assuredly testimonial, strongly indicates that in this one case an exception occurred: the dead Jesus did rise.   This is surprising, but the testimony of the witnesses shows that they were at least as surprised as we are.

Improbable though this is, all the alternative explanations of the data are even more improbable.   Clearly something quite extraordinary happened shortly after the death of Jesus to the large group of men and women who had gathered around him.   Clearly they described it as seeing the risen Jesus.   If this didn't happen, that is, if they didn't see the risen Jesus, then we must conclude that some other event or events, which no one has ever described, occurred, and that the other event or events caused a radical change in the understanding, courage, and conduct of all these men and women.   So we will have replaced a single describable miracle with fifty or five hundred indescribable miracles. We will then have to explain why, and how, this large group would've concocted a uniform and deceptive story of appearances of the risen Jesus and would've maintained that conspiracy of deception to their deaths.

There are some very fine Christian theologians, Hans Küng and Roger Haight among them, who do not accept the physical raising of Jesus in the body, but do accept that the disciples and followers of Jesus did in some way experience the living Jesus after his death, that this experience radically and permanently transformed their under-standing, their courage, and their subsequent conduct, and that this experience was the work of God.   So I conclude that it's possible to doubt the historical assertion that Jesus physically rose from the dead and still believe that God worked through an event or experience of the disciples which we can't describe.   As we've seen, Jesus himself placed great emphasis on the acceptance and practice of his ethical teachings, and he said very little about matters of belief, so I think we should allow considerable latitude toward our fellow Christians in matters of belief, even belief in the physical resurrection of Jesus.

But I personally can't get comfortable with the view that the resurrection of Jesus is symbolic, not literal, and I don't have a problem with the physical resurrection of Jesus.   I'm skeptical about miracles, but I don't have an *a priori* conviction that they can't occur.   On the basis of the historical evidence, and the extreme implausibility of any other explanation, I conclude that Jesus was somehow raised from the dead and that he subsequently appeared numerous times to his disciples. I arrive at this conclusion not by making an act or leap of faith, but as a reasonable conclusion about a historical fact based on the circumstances, on the evidence, and on my life experience.

When the risen Jesus had completed his instructions to his disciples over a period of time, perhaps forty days, he appeared at a gathering with a large group of disciples. He bade them farewell, and after that he was not seen again in the flesh on this world. Luke reports that his disciples saw him lift up into the air and disappear into a cloud (Lk 24:50-51; Acts 1:9). Well, that's as good an explanation as any.

Notes and Sources for Further Reading

For René Girard's treatment of the crucifixion of Jesus, see his *Things Hidden Since the Foundation of the World* (Stanford University Press, 1987), pp. 141-262. For his treatment of the concept of the scapegoat sacrifice, see his *The Scapegoat* (Johns Hopkins University Press, 1986).

A fine, scholarly, and important book on the question of whether the death of Jesus was a sacrifice is that of S. Mark Heim, *Saved From Sacrifice: a Theology of the Cross* (Eerdmans, 2006).

For Hans Küng's explanation of the resurrection, see *On Being a Christian* (Doubleday Image Books, 1976), pp. 343-381.

For Roger Haight's explanation of the resurrection, see *Jesus Symbol of God* (Orbis Books, 1999), pp. 119-151.

N. T. Wright's exhaustive and scholarly treatment of the resurrection of Jesus is found in his *The Resurrection of the Son of God* (Fortress Press, 2003). While Wright's book, at 738 pages, is a rather full treatment of the subject, the last 150 pages or so (pp. 587-737) contain his careful analysis and interpretation of the scriptural testimony of the resurrection and a full and persuasive argument for its historical accuracy.

VII

THE FIVE COMMANDMENTS IN PERSONAL LIFE

*"Those who love me will keep my word, and my Father will love them,
and we will come to them and make our abode with them." (Jn 14:23)*

WE NOW TURN TO A STUDY of each of the five commandments of Jesus,
in this chapter as they apply to our personal lives, and in the next as
they apply to social and political institutions. A discussion of specifically Christian teachings about God and Jesus will be deferred until
Chapter 9. I have two reasons for putting things in this order.

First, the ethical teachings of Jesus are broader than Christianity.
They are addressed to all human beings, and they address universal
human problems. It's not unlikely that someone who studies the five
commandments may conclude that Jesus was a brilliant ethical teacher
and that his five commandments are a singularly deep and difficult set
of ethical directions, penetrating in their understanding of the human
condition. It's entirely possible that the same person may have no
interest in becoming a Christian, either because he or she is unable or
unwilling to accept central Christian teachings, or simply because he or
she finds that the non-ethical teachings and practices of the Christian
churches fill no apparent need, or serve no apparent purpose, in his or
her life.

This would generally be the case for serious adherents of other
religious traditions and faiths – Islamic, Buddhist, Hindu, and others –
who have no interest in or inclination toward Christianity, but who
have an interest in and can recognize an important body of ethical
teachings which is relevant to their situations. It would be important,
and a major step forward, if some leaders and teachers within other
religious traditions would study and reflect upon the five commandments of Jesus as a set of ethical principles, and would find and
emphasize such parallel teachings in their own traditions as can be
interpreted to counsel the same conduct and serve the same purposes.
An important historical example of this is Gandhi's teaching of the
Hindu virtue of *ahimsa*, or nonviolence, which was influenced in part by
his reading of the Sermon on the Mount.

Second, what really matters for humanity and for each one of us is how each of us acts toward our fellow humans, either alone or in concert with others. Belief is secondary to action. It's how we act toward others that shows whether our beliefs are sound, whether we have sufficiently grasped the truth of things. Worship is also secondary to action. It's not how we act toward God or how we pray to God that determines whether we're leading good lives, but how we act toward other human beings, using our freedom and creativity to do good to others. This is what really determines each person's distinctive character and merit.

This is the lesson of the parable of the Last Judgment (Mt 25:31-46), which addresses the question: how is God going to look on the whole of human history to determine which people are to be saved? The answer Jesus gave in that parable is that it depends upon what each of us did for other human beings who were hungry, thirsty, alone, or mistreated. What we believed, or how we worshiped, isn't a factor. The author of the first epistle of John says, "Beloved, since God loved us so much, we also ought to love one another" (1 Jn 4:11). Note that he does not say that since God loved us so much, we ought to love God. No; the right response to God's love for us is our love for other human beings. Jesus illustrated this priority of moral action over correct expression of belief in his parable of the two sons:

> "What do you think? A man had two sons; he went to the first and said, 'Son, go and work in the vineyard today.' He answered, 'I will not'; but later he changed his mind and went. The father went to the second and said the same; and he answered, 'I go, sir'; but he did not go. Which of the two did the will of his father?" They said, "The first." (Mt 21:28-31)

The five commandments of Jesus are our essential guide to doing good for one another. The ten commandments of Moses and the natural law aren't enough. They aren't a sufficient guide for our active and practical expression of love of one another. They don't speak directly against our genetically based anti-social behaviors. They don't speak to our conscious cultivation of mental attitudes necessary to develop the virtues required for the moral life. And they don't speak against the evils absorbed by and internalized in our public institutions. The five commandments of Jesus do.

As you'll recall from the discussion in Chapter 3, Christian ethics has traditionally consisted of identifying and avoiding personal sin. The practice of the five commandments of Jesus is different. The five commandments of Jesus set forth habits to be learned, virtues to be cultivated, ideals to be striven for. They constitute virtue ethics, not penal ethics. The concept of sin just isn't helpful when it comes to changing bad habits and developing and strengthening good ones.

Consider, for example, a situation in which you're dealing with a person of a different ethnic or racial heritage. I recall several occasions when I was acting as a lawyer for an African-American client. I was very conscious of the racial difference between us, because we're all genetically and socially programmed to identify such differences and to be wary of those who are different from us. So I made a special effort not to exclude my client from my ordinary good will and good manners because of his race. But making the effort itself, while thinking about the difference, caused me to act in a more guarded, closed, or formal way, and this I think made my client uncomfortable about the difference between us. Who can say whether our personal interaction succeeded or failed? Who can say whether there has been sin? The concept of sin isn't useful. The task with all of the five commandment virtues is to go forward, clumsily but persistently, and gradually, through practice and reflection, work closer to the ideal.

Virtue ethics is like that. It's not a matter of conforming to rules; it's a matter of building good habits. It requires not obedience, but reflection, practice against resistance, and from time to time courage. Each of us knows some good people among our friends, relatives, and acquaintances who are naturally, it seems, forgiving, tolerant, humble, and peaceable, but also firm and resolute. We can follow their example, and in due course we will gradually improve.

One thing we must be aware of in studying the application of the five commandments in personal life is their presence or absence in customary social practice. Generally accepted rules of conduct in our society sometimes embody a good deal of one or another of the five commandments, but their application is spotty. For example, the United States is generally a tolerant society, and it's good, and great progress, that in 2008 most Americans were comfortable with a white woman and an African-American man as candidates for president. But much of America does not extend that tolerance to undocumented immigrants or to gays and lesbians.

Let's now review each of the five commandments to see how they work and how they are relevant to our own lives in this modern world.

Non-Judging. We begin with the first commandment, *Do not judge, blame, condemn, or exclude anyone from your fellowship and love.*

Here, as we'll see with forgiveness, we have barriers in our own minds against another person, or another group of people. Unlike forgiveness, which is required when someone has done an offense toward us, or when we've offended another, non-judging is required all the time. It takes a lifetime of work to learn it.

One reason non-judging is so difficult is that "judging," determining who is the stranger, the alien, the different one, the enemy, is a genetically based behavior and a socially and culturally reinforced behavior as well. In primitive humans, hominids, primates, and many other animals, knowing how to tell friend from foe was a valuable and often a survival skill. In primitive humans, identification with the family, the tribe, or the clan was important for preservation of the primitive community. In modern civilizations, loyalty, cooperation, and teamwork are among the most prized virtues, all the way from a pickup basketball team to the national government. To reinforce these virtues, every settled organization has its team song, from the high school fight song to the national anthem, and most religious groups have whole books of hymns, different hymn books for different denominations.

Juan Luis Segundo described our instinctive practice of "judging" this way:

> Our fidelity to Christ's great commandment is not going to show up so much with respect to persons who are bound to me by some imposed proximity. It is going to show up in our acceptance or refusal of the innumerable possibilities of establishing these relationships in the society where we live.
> So then the question is: What technique or mechanism do we use to put others at a distance, to avoid drawing near to those who are around us in our everyday world? Sociologically speaking, the answer is not difficult. In the concrete we put others at a distance by putting labels on them, by cataloguing them in neat little pigeonholes.

All of us derive our personal identities, at least in part, from our identity groups. Race, religion, nationality, social class, gender, and color all define us. I am a white male American of western European heritage (Irish, German, French), raised Catholic, now Episcopalian, married, with children and grandchildren, and a retired corporate lawyer. Now you know all about me. You have me in a pigeonhole. It's so easy and so natural to identify with our own identity groups, and to feel strangers, not neighbors, to those who share few or none of these groupings with us. It's only a small step to find ourselves treating the "other" as so different as to be mistrusted, feared, or despised. Ethnic jokes become ethnic slurs; inter-ethnic rivalries become inter-ethnic hatred.

We live in a tolerant society. Discrimination on the grounds of race, religion, national origin, gender, age, handicap, and sexual orientation is forbidden by law. And most of us have formed the habit of keeping disparaging thoughts about others to ourselves, or only sharing them with close friends or family. Isn't that enough? No, we all know that isn't enough. Ethnic, religious, and racial prejudice are still major problems in our society because we haven't set out to work on changing our minds. The first step is to understand the magnitude of the challenge, to realize that true tolerance and acceptance of all our fellow humans goes contrary to our genetically based behaviors and our deeply-seated cultural habits, and to see that constant and persistent effort needs to be made to change these behaviors and habits.

Another reason non-judging is difficult is that thinking itself requires judging of a kind: discriminating, classifying, processing data, sorting and organizing our thoughts. We habitually and automatically make judgments about people we live with, meet casually, or only read about. We need to practice the skill of being mentally aware of the subtle unfavorable judgments we almost automatically make about other people or groups. Once we feel ourselves making a semi-automatic negative judgment, we need to identify it as such and look at it thoughtfully. Then it can be evaluated and discarded if it is without merit. In this way, the practice of recognizing and second-guessing our prejudices will become habitual, and that's a great step in learning how to be non-judging. (The same kind of mental care and attention is needed to develop the virtue of humility.)

Let's illustrate the practice of non-judging by supposing you are introduced to a person described to you as a Muslim, or as a radical Islamist. Jesus said, "Love your enemies." I don't think he meant,

"See your enemies out there and love them anyway." He meant rather that we should never regard any other person as simply an "enemy." Another person is first and foremost a human person worthy of my fellowship and love. If that person himself or herself is attacking my family, my city, or my nation at the moment, obviously the need to defend my own (nonviolently, of course) takes priority. But just because the "radical Islamist" is a person of a different faith or ethnicity, with fundamentalist training or education, we can't therefore call him or her an enemy.

Beware of and distrust anyone, even the President of the United States, who tells you that there are enemies out there, many of them, with implacable hatred against "us," who are seeking our destruction. That's oversimplification on a comic book level, and a leader who uses that kind of rhetoric is simply trying to enhance his own power as leader of a group united by fear and hatred. It's the oldest trick in the book. Non-judging, like forgiveness, means removing the barriers against others in our own minds. The desired result isn't to see other people through rose-colored glasses but to see them more clearly, as individuals, as people with histories and families, as well as members, like ourselves, of identity groups. Thomas Merton stated the point well:

> Violence rests on the assumption that the enemy and I are entirely different: the enemy is evil and I am good. But love sees things differently. It sees that even the enemy suffers from the same sorrows and limitations that I do. That we both have the same hopes, the same needs, the same aspirations for a peaceful and harmless human life. And that death is the same for both of us.

It'll take more progress in seeing things this way than most of us have so far achieved to be able to see that Timothy McVeigh and Mohammad Atta had "the same hopes, the same needs, the same aspirations for a peaceful and harmless human life" as we do. But that's the goal. We know from everything Jesus said that that's how he would have seen it.

An aid to learning not to judge is often found in our working lives, where the habit of non-judging is a practical necessity. Professional people, like doctors, lawyers, and teachers, take their patients, clients, and students as they come. Corporate employees deal with customers, suppliers, and fellow employees, none of whom they choose. It's part of living in the world to learn to keep our adverse judgments about other people to ourselves, to be courteous and helpful, and to serve the needs of those with whom we deal.

Our lives in the working world often require that we get to know our clients, patients, students, or customers on a personal basis and to learn something about their lives. This is how we take another person out of his or her pigeonhole and make him or her a real person for us. When we do, this generally teaches us that most people, when you get to know them, are likeable, and many are admirable. The group identities of these people come to be simply part of their personal histories, not ways of classifying or judging them. There was an interesting poll published in the New York Times a few years ago. In it some 57% of those polled said that they disapproved of marriage or civil unions for gays and lesbians. The poll also found that some 57% of those polled believed that they didn't know personally anyone who was gay or lesbian. Need I say more?

Forgiveness. We proceed to the second commandment, *Forgive all who have offended you.*

Forgiveness is complicated because it's the resolution of a complex situation. We must look at forgiveness from two points of view, that of the person forgiving and that of the person receiving forgiveness. Jesus spoke of both as closely related and intertwined when he said, "Forgive, and you will be forgiven" (Lk 6:37). But they are not the same.

Take a simple example. Al and his wife invite her sister and her sister's husband Bill for dinner. At dinner, Al's six-year-old son spills his milk, and it splashes on Bill's trousers. Bill, who is having a bad day, yells at Al that he should discipline his children better. Al protests, but Bill goes into a tirade, sweeps his arm across the table in his anger, breaking some china, and storms out of the house. (I've simplified the example to show Bill in the wrong; in real life, it's more often mixed.)

Now what's going on in the minds of Al and Bill? Al is angry at Bill and doesn't know if he and Bill can ever get along again. He has a barrier in his mind against Bill. Bill is trying without much success to justify his actions to himself. He holds on to his anger against Al, and at the same time he tries to excuse himself: he was having a bad day, Al's kid was not fit for the adult table, and so forth. And he realizes that he may never again be welcomed in his brother-in-law's home. So he has a barrier in his mind against Al. Diagrammatically, it looks like this:

Forgiving one | barrier || barrier | Forgiven one

For forgiveness to be completed, each party must remove the barrier in his mind. Each party is responsible only for removing the barrier in his own mind and can't do the other's job.

Al must first acknowledge, and then let go of, his anger against Bill and recall his general respect for and affection for Bill. He must deal with and reject the false responses: the desire to retaliate in some way, and the desire to exclude Bill from the family or at least from the accustomed friendship between them. He must resist the temptation to forgive conditionally, which would make any forgiveness from him conditional on Bill's apology, repentance, or restitution. Offering conditional forgiveness is partly forgiveness and partly an attempt to control. If Al puts conditions on his forgiveness of Bill, he is justifying in his own mind the righteousness of the barrier in his own mind against Bill. Only when we forgive unconditionally does the barrier dissolve.

This simple example shows how closely interwoven the five commandments are and how they act together. To forgive, Al must reject condemning Bill in his own mind, or shunning or excluding him in the future (thus non-judging). He must reject retaliation of any kind, particularly violent retaliation (nonviolence). He must reject self-righteousness and empathize with Bill (humble service). And he mustn't be too upset about the broken china (detachment from possessions).

Bill has a different set of tasks and a different kind of barrier in his own mind to remove. He must see his actions for what they were, indefensible, but not unforgivable. He must recognize his fault, apologize, repair the damages, and ask for forgiveness, which takes humility, which is here, as in most cases, simply a realistic self-image. If he's unable to see that he was at fault, or unable to live with himself as a person with flaws, he won't be able to accept forgiveness, and the barrier against Al will remain in his mind.

The God of the Hebrew Scriptures was (most of the time) a controlling God, with a barrier against Israel in his divine mind. His anger and wrath were quick, and his forgiveness slow and always conditional. In their way of looking at things, the Israelites believed that God exercised control over human conduct by punishment, so any human misfortune was often taken as a sign of God's punishment. When Jesus and his disciples saw a man blind since birth, they asked him, "Rabbi, who sinned, this man or his parents, that he was born blind?" (Jn 9:2).

It's a new teaching from Jesus that God forgives unconditionally and gratuitously. This means that there's no barrier to forgiveness on God's side. The only thing necessary to make God's forgiveness complete is that we remove the barrier in our own minds and accept God's forgiveness. The message of the parables of the Prodigal Son (Lk 15:11-32) and of the Pharisee and the Publican (Lk 18:9-14) is that God's forgiveness is gratuitous, always available, and always unconditional.

Nonviolence. We turn to the third commandment, *Do not do violence to any person, even in response to violence.*

This is the point at which some people abandon the teachings of Jesus. He'll turn us all into meek victims of violence, they say. We need to be able to defend ourselves with violent resistance, and avenge our injuries with violent retaliation, or we'll be ruled by the bad guys. We need our guns.

These views are instinctive. They're fixed in our genes. But because we all live in societies with functioning criminal justice systems, these views are false. Cultural anthropology and common experience have taught us two things about private violence: that it's reciprocal and that it inevitably escalates. An all-too-common scenario in our society illustrates this: Late at night, in a bar, or in someone's house, a bunch of guys have been drinking too much. One insults another, the other shoves back, and the two start swinging at each other. One is driven out of the bar or the house. He goes to his car, or his own house, gets a gun, and comes back and shoots the other. If the police don't arrive quickly, friends or relatives of the slain victim go for their guns, shoot back at the assailant and his friends, and reciprocal violence escalates. If the victim is a gang member, or of a tight and lawless family, his co-members seek out and assault members of the assailant's group the next day, or the next week, and a small private war begins. The tragedy of violent retaliation and its escalation is as old as *Romeo and Juliet* and as new as this morning's newspaper. And we don't have the ritual blood sacrifice to bring it under control.

Jesus saw that this was, and would continue to be, the way of humans, and he forbade violent defense and violent revenge. But he didn't counsel submission or passivity. He didn't see the instinctive alternatives, fight or flight, as the only alternatives. He taught that we must respond to violence counter-instinctively, with nonviolent resistance. Walter Wink explains this in his reading of the key passage in Matthew, where Jesus said,

> You have heard that it was said, "An eye for an eye and a tooth for a tooth." But I say to you, do not resist an evildoer. But if anyone strikes you on the right cheek, turn the other also; and if anyone wants to sue you and take your coat, give your cloak as well; and if anyone forces you to go one mile, go also the second mile. (Mt 5:38-41).

First, Wink explains, the phrase "Do not resist an evildoer" must be read to mean "Do not *use violence to* resist an evildoer," both because that is what the Greek word in Matthew 5:39 translated as "resist," *antistenai*, means, and because all of Jesus's illustrations of this rule are examples of nonviolent resistance. He then shows how this is so.

"If anyone strikes you on the right cheek . . ." – why the *right* cheek? A blow of the right fist, or a right-handed slap, would strike the left cheek. Only a backhand slap would hit the right cheek, and this is a gesture used to humiliate an inferior, a servant, a peasant, or a slave, not to start a fight with an equal. By turning the left cheek toward the striker, the servant takes away the power of the oppressor to humiliate him with another backhand blow. Try it: you'll see.

"If anyone sues you and takes your coat, give your cloak as well." Jesus is describing a legal process of foreclosing on a debtor so poor that he has no collateral but the clothes on his back, a custom common in Israel, and regulated in the Hebrew Scriptures. See Exodus 22:25-27 and Deuteronomy 24:10-13. Jesus counsels that the victim of such an unjust procedure, when ordered to surrender his outer garment, give up the rest of his clothes as well, as a protest against the system which has rendered him destitute, and by so doing shame the creditor and the officers of the court. (Jesus isn't wholly without a sense of humor.)

"If anyone forces you to go one mile, go also the second mile." Jesus here refers to the right of every Roman soldier to force or impress any member of a subject people to carry his pack, a right which was limited by Roman rules to one mile. Jesus counseled that an impressed Jew should resist in a nonviolent way by carrying the load an extra mile. This action would confuse the soldier. Was the Jew helping him, insulting his strength, or trying to get him into trouble? In each of these cases Jesus is showing how people of courage and imagination can resist oppression nonviolently and assert their independence by embarrassing the oppressor. Nonviolent tactics like these, intended to embarrass and shame the oppressing force and assert independence, formed a major part of the civil disobedience campaigns of Gandhi and Martin Luther King. A sit-in at a drugstore lunch counter is exactly the kind of nonviolent resistance Jesus was talking about.

Desire for violent retaliation or revenge for violence received is one of the strongest of human passions. I had a revealing conversation with my legal assistant on September 11, 2002, the first anniversary of the terrorist bombings of September 11, 2001. "The hardest Christian doctrine to accept," I suggested, "is that human life survives death." "No," she replied, "the hardest Christian doctrine to accept is nonviolence. We want so much to retaliate and get revenge." I think she was right. As Jesus pointed out, even the Hebrew Scriptures approved the practice of vengeful retaliation in an ineffective effort to restrain the escalation of violence: "If any harm follows, then you shall give life for life, eye for eye, tooth for tooth, hand for hand, foot for foot, burn for burn, stripe for stripe" (Exod 21:23-25; Lev 24:19-20; Deut 19:21). But once reciprocal violence begins, it inevitably escalates.

A striking example of the persistence, escalation and attraction of retaliatory violence was recounted by Jared Diamond in an April 2008 issue of the New Yorker magazine. Diamond tells the story of Daniel Wemp, a young member of the Handa clan of the New Guinea Highland people. Daniel's uncle had been killed in a battle with the neighboring Ombal clan, and it was Daniel's duty to arrange the revenge. The war between the Handa and the Ombal, which had been going on for as long as Daniel could remember, had started because of a pig that ruined a garden. It took Daniel three years of battles, in which twenty-nine men were killed, to discharge his responsibility for revenge. In the sixth and decisive battle between Handa and Ombal, the "owner" of the earlier battle in which Daniel's uncle was killed was himself shot in the spine with a bamboo arrow and paralyzed. After the battle, Daniel described his feelings:

> When you fight with thinking and finally succeed, you feel good and relieved. The revenge relieves you; now it can be your turn to help someone else get his own revenge.

Reciprocal violence necessarily involves breaking four of the five commandments of Jesus. In order to do violence, we must first exclude the intended victim of our violence from the group to whom we owe human respect and care. We must condemn and demonize the victim. This is the key element in the training of combat soldiers and of war propaganda generally. Anyone committing violent retaliation must exclude and condemn the victim, consider himself superior to the victim, and deny him or her forgiveness, before taking revenge. If you begin to think of a person, a group of people, or all members of an ethnic or religious group, as your enemy, stop and think. That's a sign that you are departing from the teachings of Jesus.

Humble Service. The fourth commandment of Jesus is *Act as a humble servant toward all others.*

This commandment teaches the fundamental equality of all human persons. It's always easy to persuade yourself that you or your identity group are superior in initiative, or diligence, or courage, or any of a number of virtues, to others outside the group. Jesus particularly singled out and condemned the attitude of feeling morally or spiritually superior, in his frequent harsh reproaches to the Pharisees. However, Jesus thought it would make sense for us to use our pride to develop our humility. I had a friend in college who announced one day that he wanted to be an intellectual, and that he would first become a pseudo-intellectual, in the hope that it would sink in. Similarly, in the parable of the one who took the higher place at table (Lk 14:8-11), Jesus counsels that to serve your prideful desire to avoid public humiliation and to win public honor, you should take the lower place, and thus learn to practice humility from the outside in.

Life, to Jesus, isn't a zero-sum game. He preached that God loves everyone and that, as we're blessed by God's love, we should never be concerned whether God seems to love someone else more, or less. "The last will be first, and the first will be last," Jesus repeatedly said. This is the lesson of the parable of the workers in the field who were hired at different times of day and paid the same wage (Mt 20:1-16). I suggest that this means not only that we don't know in what state we will end up as compared with others, but also that Jesus is saying that it doesn't matter. Comparisons with others about who is more loved by God are without meaning and usually invidious, and we ought to repress them as useless distractions.

Jesus taught that the only way we can reach a settled feeling of equality with all others is to act as a humble servant toward everyone else. This means listening to, caring for, and giving respect to everyone with whom we deal. "All who exalt themselves will be humbled, and those who humble themselves will be exalted." This attitude of humble service, based on the doctrine that "all men are created equal," is an essential support to the performance of the first three commandments. An attitude of superiority is a kind of judging and excluding others. Humility is necessary for us to see others as they truly are and to approach them in fellowship. Humble service aids forgiveness. We can forgive if we see ourselves as also needing forgiveness from time to time. And a humble person doesn't hate and thus do violence to another person.

A great help in learning humble service can be found in working with others, either in our jobs, working with partners and fellow employees, or in an active role with a charitable, political, or civic committee or activity. My own experience practicing law was that I often went into a planning meeting with a definite plan and came out, humbled, but with a much changed and improved plan, which reflected the contributions of the others in the meeting. Among the joys of my practice in a partnership was my routine of consulting my partners on questions upon which they had greater expertise, or better judgment, than I, and helping my partners when they consulted me for the same purpose. This practice usually improved the result for my clients and theirs. I've long enjoyed singing in choirs and choruses, in humble servitude to the music director. Working with good people in groups does good things for your humility. Working as a volunteer, feeding the poor in a soup kitchen, ministering to those in prison, and caring for the sick and handicapped are good actions of good people who are practicing humility and humble service.

The commandment of humble service speaks directly against dominant-submissive behaviors. Men are not to dominate women.

Wives are not to be submissive to husbands. Each should serve the other with humility. The followers of Jesus included both men and women, and he frequented the company of people of high and low reputation and esteem. Holders of an office or profession, such as teachers, doctors, lawyers, corporate managers, and government officials, have the authority in their respective fields to give instructions and orders as well as advice to their pupils, patients, and other subordinates. But those with such authority have a special duty to act as humble servants to those subject to their authority.

My father died in 1981, nine years after he had retired from his office as a vice president of a Cleveland bank. I remember his funeral. None of the bank officers he had worked for or reported to came to the funeral, but the people who had worked for him came, and spoke highly of him to me. My father, I think, had been a humble servant to those who were subject to his authority.

Similarly, the commandment of humble service proscribes hierarchies. Human organizations need leaders, and often several levels of leadership, to function and to perform their assigned tasks. But leaders are not elevated into a superior class of people by reason of their offices. They must remain in some real sense the servants of those they lead, and in most organizations and communities they should be chosen by, and subject to removal by, the members of their communities. It's particularly important in religious organizations that those called to ministry observe the commandment of humble service. The call to ministry, or the ordination or consecration of a bishop, a minister, or a priest, doesn't elevate the bishop, priest, or minister to a superior moral position or a superior state of life.

Detachment from Possessions. We finally reach the fifth commandment of Jesus, *Detach yourself from possessions.*

This commandment requires a carefully nuanced understanding. Nearly all Christians, like nearly all people, live in the world, not in monasteries or convents. To live in the world requires the ownership and use of possessions. Jesus didn't counsel or teach renunciation of possessions, except for a very few whom he called to that life. The task for nearly all of us is to own and use possessions without becoming attached to them and to make the use of possessions subordinate to the practice of moral virtues.

Jesus said, referring to food and clothes, "Your heavenly Father knows that you need all these things. But strive first for the kingdom of God and his righteousness, and all these things will be given to you as well" (Mt 6:32-33; Lk 12:30-31). In Chapter 5 I argued that the kingdom of God is the community of those who practice his five commandments. So Jesus is saying that if we practice his five commandments, and if we subordinate the acquisition of possessions to this practice, we will be striving first for the kingdom of God, and the necessary possessions will be provided. He didn't mean that God will provide for us in lieu of our own natural initiative, attention, persistence, and hard work. He may have meant that the thoughtful, perceptive, and reflective habits we develop in working to understand and put into practice his commandments will aid us in acquiring and using possessions with prudence, restraint, and economy. The history of modern Europe and North America gives some indication that in broad terms this is the case.

What is to be resisted is obsession with acquisitions, possessions, and display of wealth. Here the modern middle classes in developed countries have an advantage over the rich and the poor. Our available money, prudently managed, is sufficient for a reasonably comfortable life but is limited, so that obsessive imbalance or excess in its use is usually self-correcting. The rich are not protected by this practical limitation. The poor don't have the security of regular money and are more vulnerable to obsession with goods, because even the necessary minimums are so hard to obtain. But all of us are vulnerable to obsession with money and goods and have to deal with the problem of governing and balancing our needs and desires with the available money every day of our lives.

* * * * *

I've identified the five commandments of Jesus and I've discussed the practice of the virtues they prescribe. Implicit in my thesis that the practice of these particular virtues constitutes and builds the kingdom of God on earth is the assertion that these virtues are central to the moral life, and that the many other virtues of a moral life are either subsumed in the practice of these virtues or are provided for in another way. Without making an exhaustive examination of all possible virtues, let's examine some familiar sets of virtues to see whether or not this is the case.

Let's take first the so-called "cardinal virtues," prudence, justice, fortitude, and temperance. These are simply the virtues of human maturity. Their practice is the mark of a person who has reached responsible adulthood in an organized civil society. These are the virtues which make the present world livable, not the virtues which change the world. They're sufficiently inculcated and enforced by the practical social and civil consequences of failure.

Take the second tablet commandments of Moses: Thou shalt not kill, commit adultery, steal, bear false witness, or covet thy neighbor's wife or goods. These are prohibitions against conduct which does grievous harm to the fabric of any society, and most of them are prohibited by law in every civilization. The elaboration and extension of the second tablet commandments in the Episcopal Book of Common Prayer, p. 848, is a noble and sound compendium of Judaeo-Christian virtues:

Q.   What is our duty to our neighbors?
A.   Our duty to our neighbors is to love them as ourselves, and to do to other people as we wish them to do to us;
   V   To love, honor and help our parents and family; to honor those in authority, and to meet their just demands;
   VI   To show respect for the life God has given us; to work and pray for peace; to bear no malice, prejudice, or hatred in our hearts; and to be kind to all the creatures of God;
   VII   To use all our bodily desires as God intended;
   VIII   To be honest and fair in our dealings; to seek justice, freedom, and the necessities of life for all peoples; and to use our talents and possessions as ones who must answer for them to God;
   IX   To speak the truth, and not to mislead others by our silence;
   X   To resist temptations to envy, greed, and jealousy; to rejoice in other people's gifts and graces; and to do our duty for the love of God, who has called us into fellowship with him.

There are several allusions to the five commandments of Jesus in this extension of the ten commandments: "Bear no malice, prejudice or hatred in our hearts" is non-judging, in a way. "Use our talents and possessions as ones who must answer for them to God" is close to the point of detachment from possessions. But generally, this elaboration is unfocused.

The five commandments of Jesus have, above all, focus. Each zeroes in on a specific constant genetically based source of human weakness. The fact that the practice of each commandment requires constant work, constant vigilance, and regular practice against resistance is an important part of their focus. Their practice is a daily chore, but the habits formed by such practice are the ethical foundation of the true followers of Jesus. The five commandments are bound together as very specific directions for following the New Commandment of Jesus, which summarizes all the others: "Love one another." It's these specific directions which make the New Commandment new. The command to love one another is implicit in the first of the five commandments of Jesus: *Do not judge, blame, condemn, or exclude any person from your fellowship and love.* So it seems clear to me that those of us who can live the life demanded by the five commandments of Jesus will, in the process, have developed all the other ethical virtues required for a virtuous moral life.

Learning how to practice the five commandments and how to make their practice habitual needs to be supported by prayer. Two forms of prayer are particularly suitable for this purpose. The first is the regular, slow, and contemplative reading of the Gospels. This practice deepens our understanding of the five commandments and of Jesus, the person who taught us the commandments and then showed us in his life and death how they should be lived. The second is regular meditation in one of its many forms: centering prayer, yoga, or the ways of the great mystics and contemplative monks and nuns. Regular meditation in any of these classical forms brings us into contact with the presence of God within us, whether this is called the ground of being, the *atman*, or the God-consciousness. I'll have more to say about the God-consciousness in Chapter 9.

We turn now to the question whether, and how, the five commandments can be applied to the social, cultural, and political institutions of our society.

Notes and Sources for Further Reading

Terrence J. Rynne's book, *Gandhi and Jesus: the Saving Power of Nonviolence* (Orbis Books, 2008), is a fine comparison of the ethics of Gandhi with the ethics of Jesus.

A discussion of virtue ethics, as distinguished from penal ethics, is found in Daniel Harrington's and John F. Keenan's book, *Jesus and Virtue Ethics: Building Bridges Between New Testament Studies and Moral Theology* (Rowman & Littlefield, 2002), pp. 23-31.

The quotation from Juan Luis Segundo is from *Our Idea of God* (Orbis Books, 1974), p. 113.

I found the quotation from Thomas Merton in an article in *The New York Times*, October 21, 2001, p. A-16.

Walter Wink's reading of the passage from Matthew on nonviolence is found in *Engaging the Powers* (Fortress Press, 1992), pp. 175-89.

Diamond's article is *Vengeance Is Ours,* The New Yorker, April 21, 2008, p. 74.

On the positive association between Christian virtues and prosperity, see R. H. Tawney, *Religion and the Rise of Capitalism* (Mentor Books, 1947).

VIII

The Five Commandments in Public Life

"God sent not his Son into the world to condemn the world;
but that the world through him might be saved." (Jn 3:17)

APPLYING THE FIVE COMMANDMENTS OF JESUS to institutions of society is an idea which has rarely been tried. Before the Christian church became the official church of the Roman Empire under Constantine, Christians had no voice in government or public life, and thus no opportunity to apply the commandments to public institutions. After the Christian church became the official church, it was too closely intertwined with civil government to be deeply critical of public institutions. This tradition has continued with little change.

Even in modern times, Christian churches generally haven't preached the application of the five commandments to public life and civil institutions. Yet the attacks Jesus made against the culture of sacrifice, not only in his teaching of the five commandments, but also in his campaign against the sacrifice itself and its associated rules, rituals, and practices, all of them key components of the public and institutional life of the nation of Israel, leaves no doubt that he intended his followers to apply the five commandments in public life and to public institutions.

There have of course been attempts throughout the history of Christianity to apply various Christian moral principles to public life. Two fairly recent examples are the social teachings of the Catholic church over the last 140 years or so and the Social Gospel movement of some American Protestant churches in the early twentieth century. We can learn some lessons about what works and what doesn't work from this part of Christian history. Based in part on this history, I suggest that there are three general guidelines of Christian social action which should lead followers of Jesus away from what doesn't work and toward what does. I'll first discuss the guidelines themselves and then illustrate how they work in the discussion of each of the five commandments.

The first guideline is: *Persuasion Is Permitted But Coercion Is Not.*

A principal goal of followers of Jesus is to reform public institutions with the ultimate aim of fostering and increasing the freedom and creativity of all men and women living within these institutions. Since increasing freedom is the aim, all efforts of Christians to do so must take place in a context of expanding freedom, not in a context of coercion or power. The historical record of attempts by Christians and Christian churches to apply principles of Christian morality in the public and political spheres has often been a history of coercion, curtailing human freedom instead of expanding it, followed by failure. Indeed, these failures have been so frequent and notorious as to explain in part the present reluctance of many Christian churches to speak out on public issues, as well as the fact that many people ignore the churches when they do speak out.

There are two mistakes which have historically been made by Christians and Christian churches in trying to apply Christian moral principles in the public arena. The first error is the position that if an act is immoral in the eyes of a Christian church, it ought to be prohibited, not only in the church's religious teaching, but also by the civil or criminal law. The second mistake, close to the first, is that if certain good conduct is morally required in the eyes of a Christian church, it's therefore permissible and often appropriate to use the coercive powers of the state to compel its performance.

Historical examples of coercion to achieve religious goals are many. Among the best known are the Spanish Inquisition, the civil government of Geneva during the time of John Calvin, and the burning first of Catholic heretics and then of Protestant heretics in Tudor England. The principle of separation of church and state was developed partially in reaction to these notorious abuses of church and state power. But tendencies toward the abuse of human freedom in the name of Christian morality have survived to modern times. The Social Gospel movement inspired Jane Addams to open Hull House in Chicago, which in turn inspired many others to open settlement houses across the country, and that turned out well. But the Social Gospel movement also achieved one of its greatest successes with the passage of the Eighteenth Amendment, prohibiting the manufacture and sale of alcoholic beverages. This law was coercive, imposing a religious conviction on many who had no personal ethical objections to beer, wine, and liquor, and it didn't turn out well at all.

There are many current examples. Take the disputes about abortion. Everyone agrees that the practical question of abortion is a serious moral issue to those involved in the decision when the circumstances arise. On the face of it, it appears that the public dispute is between those who think abortion is morally grave, but sometimes permissible, and those who think it is morally grave and never permissible. But that isn't the real issue. If it were, the present state of the civil law would be satisfactory to both sides. Under present law, no woman can be required to have an abortion against her wishes or her religious convictions, and no woman is prohibited from having an abortion if that is her decision. Every woman is free to follow her conscience on the matter.

But that isn't satisfactory to the zealots who lead the anti-abortion movement. They seek to make their personal religious convictions part of the civil and criminal law, and then to require civil authorities to use the state's coercive power to make safe abortions unavailable to those whose consciences don't consider having an abortion impermissible. Thus the real issues between the parties are whether a religiously-based ethical position should be made the law of the state simply because it's strongly held as a religious view, and whether the coercive force of the state should be used to enforce a law so based. As the debate rarely discusses this real issue, it yields no light or progress, only continued heat and acrimony.

The guidelines recognize that the state (or any other secular institution, for that matter) isn't the church. Church and state have separate and independent functions. Church teachings and state laws overlap in some areas, as for example both prohibit robbery and burglary. But even in those areas they have quite different ends and purposes. Church ethical teachings are based on what the church in question perceives God's will to be. They're intended to guide men and women in their search to do God's will, to do good and avoid evil. State laws are intended to preserve and protect an orderly and secure society within a public legal and criminal justice system. The churches have no teachings about raising revenues to pay for public administration and public works or about regulating the purchase and sale of securities. The state doesn't prohibit coveting, nor does it require people to attend Mass.

After years of failure, states generally don't regulate private sexual activity between consenting adults, despite the efforts of religious groups to have the state do so. There's generally no public purpose to be served by laws governing private sexual morality, and enforcement of such laws is impossible without violation of the privacy of citizens. This doesn't mean that adultery or cohabitation without marriage are necessarily good things; it simply means that any public purpose to be served by prohibiting them isn't worth the cost of personally invasive enforcement measures, particularly when the person whose private life is invaded doesn't consider that the prohibited conduct is wrong. The same should be true of abortion. Coercion by state power isn't a Christian way to achieve a faith-based goal.

The second guideline is: *Use the Five Commandments of Jesus as the Principal Diagnostic Tool.*

This is what makes the social action of followers of Jesus specifically Christian. As we'll see when we examine the social application of the commandments one by one, the five commandments often help us to identify the core ethical issue in a complex and troubled social problem and to determine what kind of change is necessary to reform and redeem the institution involved.

In contrast, the social teachings of the Catholic church, as well as many of its ethical teachings, are based entirely on the natural law as understood by Catholic thinkers. This is a system of ethical philosophy. There's nothing particularly Christian about these teachings except their historical roots in the philosophical teachings of historically Catholic universities. I don't disparage them. Many principles of the Catholic social teachings are sound, noble, and helpful. But they don't bring to bear on ethical and social problems the teachings Jesus emphasized in his ministry. And thus they don't identify the root problems of institutions of the culture of sacrifice.

The third guideline is: *Only Non-Religious Arguments Are To Be Used for Advocating Reform of Secular Institutions.*

We live in secular societies. The state isn't the secular arm of the church. Political and social institutions have their own purposes, goals, and principles. Any advocacy of change in policy of a secular governmental or social institution can be legitimately supported only with arguments which relate to the purposes and goals of that institution. In the discussion of the application of each of the five commandments below, I'll first state the public institutional problem, second, use the commandment to diagnose the problem, and third, develop a secular policy analysis. The arguments for change in public policy made in each secular policy analysis all relate to the purposes and goals of the public institution in question. Only these arguments are appropriate for use in the public sphere.

For example, it isn't a legitimate argument against the over-militarization of the United States in general, or against the waging of any war in particular, to say that Jesus teaches nonviolence. It is a legitimate argument to assert that the size of the United States military establishment is much too large for any legitimate foreseeable need, or that a given war is very bad international policy, wastes the resources of the nation, hurts the legitimate interests of the nation, or violates treaties binding on the nation. The fact that the advocate of change is personally motivated by the teachings and life of Jesus is important to him or her but irrelevant to the public argument.

Barack Obama expressed this guideline well in a 2006 speech to a Sojourners/Call to Renewal conference:

> Democracy demands that the religiously motivated translate their concerns into universal, rather than religion-specific, values. It requires that their proposals be subject to argument, and amenable to reason. I may be opposed to abortion for religious reasons, but if I seek to pass a law banning the practice, I cannot simply point to the teachings of my church or evoke God's will. I have to explain why abortion violates some principle that is accessible to people of all faiths, including those with no faith at all.

When a religiously-motivated person, working for a change in public or institutional policy, finds support for the change he or she advocates in arguments of public policy, not of religious morality, he or she finds allies among those of different religious or no religious persuasions. This is good. This is part of the plan. Jesus spent his public life advocating, teaching, and persuading, but never coercing. And Jesus was happy with help from those who didn't follow him:

> John said to him, "Teacher, we saw someone casting out demons in your name, and we tried to stop him, because he was not following us." But Jesus said, "Do not stop him; for no one who does a deed of power in my name will be able

soon afterward to speak evil of me. Whoever is not against us is for us." (Mk 9:38-40; Lk 9:49-50)

It's interesting that "casting out demons" can be understood as a metaphor for redeeming public institutions by casting out the genetically based anti-social behaviors which they have internalized, which Walter Wink calls the "domination system" or the "powers that be," and which is just what we've been talking about.

Let's now see how each of the five commandments of Jesus may be applied to diagnose and remedy defective social, cultural, and political institutions. I'll discuss one illustrative problem for each commandment. In each case, the selected issue is certainly not the only, and perhaps not the most important, of the issues to which that commandment can be applied.

Non-judging. We begin with the first commandment, *Do not judge, blame, condemn, or exclude anyone from your fellowship and love.*

The problem of illegal or undocumented immigrants in the United States is a difficult one. Many people are passionate about the issue and at opposite poles of the debate. A reasonable solution doesn't seem to be in reach.

In the light of the five commandments of Jesus, we can see the core problem: the undocumented immigrants are being judged, blamed, and excluded from society for trying, in the only way available to them, to find work so that they can support their families. We see, in the strong opposition to legalizing their status, much of the same inter-ethnic fear and exclusion that has always played a prominent role in American history, from the "Know-Nothings" of the 1840s, to strong resistance to the most recent group of immigrants (first to the Irish, then to the Italians, the Poles, the various Slavic groups, the Russian Jews), to the present day. This inter-ethnic fear and hatred seriously exacerbates the present illegal immigrants problem and frustrates attempts to arrive at reasonable solutions. The undocumented Latin American immigrant is demonized by a very vocal American minority, many of whom seem to have forgotten their own immigrant roots.

It's helpful to look to see whether or not we have a beam in our own eye. We do. For sixty or seventy years, United States businesses, principally its agricultural, landscaping, hospitality, and construction businesses, have wanted or needed cheap and transient labor.

Satisfying this need with immigrant labor has generally been accepted by America, but the immigration laws of the nation have not been amended to take into account the fact that "illegal" immigrants are here because our businesses want them here.

When a small town establishes a ridiculously low speed limit on the highway through the town, we call it a "speed trap," criticize the township, and sympathize with the motorists caught in the trap. But when business and agriculture attract a migrant labor force from Latin America, and Congress establishes ridiculously small quotas for legal immigrants, we don't see it as a "migration trap," and sympathize with the immigrants. Instead we talk about building walls on our borders and deporting millions of people, both wholly impractical solutions. Our "know-nothings" speak loudly, and the rest of us passively acquiesce in the judging, blaming, condemning, and excluding shouts.

So the first of the five commandments tells us to include, not exclude, the illegal immigrants in our fellowship. Are there non-faith-based reasons for doing so? Certainly. They're here. We need their labor. We can't jail or deport twelve million people. But as long as they have no legal status, we can't protect them or police them either. Native workers rightly point out that immigrant workers work for less, and displace them. But a more effective remedy for that problem would be to give the immigrants legal status of some kind and then enforce the minimum wage laws, the wage-and-hour laws, and the tax withholding laws for their benefit. Then the playing field will be level.

What can a small group of followers of Jesus do in this situation? One course of action would be to join a local group which assists local immigrant communities with problems of shelter, security, and language. Another would be to organize local inter-faith and inter-ethnic dialogue groups and invite immigrants to participate. And each local group can and should make its views known to their senators and congressmen, so that a just and non-excluding legislative solution to the problem can be enacted.

Forgiveness. We turn to the second commandment, *Forgive all who have offended you.*

Consider the problem of the prison systems in the United States. The United States locks up more people altogether, and a greater proportion of its population, than any other nation. The United States imprisons more people in total than China, which has more than four times its population. Britain confines about one-fifth as much of the British population as the United States does of Americans, and Britain has the highest prison confinement rate in Europe. Conditions in many American prisons are shameful. The rate of recidivism is unacceptably high. The cost of keeping over 2.3 million people behind bars threatens to bankrupt many states.

First comes our diagnosis. If we look to the five commandments, we see that we, acting through our criminal justice systems, have refused to forgive the prisoners. Jesus didn't often speak of particular social problems, but the Gospel of Matthew records him speaking to this one:

> Then the king will say to those at his right hand, "Come, you that are blessed by my Father, inherit the kingdom prepared for you from the foundation of the world; for . . . I was in prison and you visited me." Then the righteous will answer him, "Lord, when was it that we saw you . . . in prison and visited you?" And the king will answer them, "Truly, I tell you, just as you did it to one of the least of these who are members of my family, you did it to me." (Mt 25:34, 36-37, 39-40)

Our communal refusal to forgive is a major factor in the injustices and social evils caused by our criminal justice system.

Next comes secular policy analysis. It shouldn't be the state's business to exact revenge upon the convicted criminal. The state's business is to protect the people. Imprisoning people for violent crimes they've committed is necessary, since violent persons need to be removed from the community for the protection of the people. Imprisonment for nonviolent crimes, particularly victimless crimes, is more problematical and of doubtful utility. But in all cases the goal of confinement shouldn't be punishment, but reform, rehabilitation, and education. As very few people are the same person they were twenty years before, long periods of confinement, even for very serious crimes, should be the exception. (This is the case in Europe.) Prisoners should be protected from each other while in confinement. The criminal justice system was invented to preempt private vengeance, not systematize it; to curtail violence, not simply to concentrate it.

What can a small Christian group do? Visit the imprisoned, as Jesus said. Volunteer for a group which teaches in prisons, or works on resettlement and re-entry problems for those who have served their time. Help create and maintain correction and rehabilitation programs which are an alternative to imprisonment. Christian groups should support elected legislators in working for reduced sentences, advocating repeal of the draconian and counter-productive provisions of our drug laws, and providing adequate funding for alternative correction and rehabilitation programs.

Nonviolence. We turn next to the third commandment, *Do not do violence to any person, even in response to violence.*

A particular problem of the United States is its inclination, under many administrations, but particularly under the last one, to treat war as an instrument of policy rather than of defense. Our military forces extend American power around the globe, at immense cost in lives lost or broken, and in expense which has made the United States the world's largest debtor nation. The United States spends more money on its military forces than all the rest of the nations of the world combined. Given the self-perpetuating power of the American military-industrial complex, there seems to be no hope for change in this pattern. American military power has long been divorced from the purpose of defense. In none of the wars of the last sixty years has the use of American military power been justified by an attack or even a credible threat of attack on United States soil, with the sole exception of the attacks of September 11, 2001, after which our military power was misdirected.

First comes the diagnosis. The commandment of Jesus is to refrain from violence, particularly retaliatory violence. If this applies to nations, as I argue it does, it certainly applies to the United States, which holds itself out as a Christian nation.

Jesus particularly singled out retaliatory violence for good reason. Perhaps the most powerful emotion felt by humans is the desire to retaliate with violence against a violent attack. The desire for revenge is such a strong emotion that it often overrides rational thinking about the consequences of revenge. If we reflect on it, it's clear that the real reason the United States invaded and at the time of this writing still occupies Iraq is the desire of the American public for revenge for the attacks of September 11, 2001. Weapons of mass destruction had little to do with the decision to go to war in Iraq. We didn't even wait for the U.N. inspectors to finish looking for them. Bringing democracy to the Iraqis was never a real reason, nor was the fact that Saddam Hussein was an evil ruler; there are undemocratic states and evil rulers all over the world. President Bush continually asserted that the war in Iraq was part of the war against al Qaeda, despite the continued absence of any credible evidence that Iraq or the Saddam regime had ever had anything to do with al Qaeda. It's hard to believe that if the attacks of September 11 had never happened, the Bush administration would have pushed so hard for the invasion of Iraq or that Congress would have approved the invasion.

Why Iraq, which had nothing to do with 9/11? Because Afghanistan was too small and too far away, and because Saudi Arabia, where fifteen of the nineteen September 11 hijackers came from, was too important to our oil supply and too close to the Bush family. The President, our mimetic leader, had the power to tell us who the enemy is, and he chose Iraq. Because revenge, which overrides clear planning, was the driving emotion of the Bush administration and the American people, that emotion took over, and rational planning for the occupation didn't take place, as subsequent events have so clearly and tragically shown.

We proceed to the secular policy analysis. Are there sound secular policy reasons for changing our minds and reducing our national use of violence as policy? There are.

Violent revenge as a public policy is fatally flawed. The incendiary bombings of Hamburg, Dresden and Tokyo in the Second World War had no military effect. They were acts of revenge, as are bombings of civilian targets generally. The atomic bombings of Hiroshima and Nagasaki were acts of revenge for Japanese atrocities, pure and simple. Within a few days of those bombings, the United States and Japan agreed on terms of surrender which the Japanese government had offered a month earlier.

Is nonviolence a tenable alternative? Most people would say no. But the evidence is to the contrary. Look at the following list of changes in regime since the end of the Second World War:

Year	Nonviolent Changes of Regime	Violent Changes of Regime
1947	India	China
1953		Iran

Year	Nonviolent Changes of Regime	Violent Changes of Regime
1954		Guatemala
1957	Ghana	
1953-75		Vietnam
1973		Chile
1974	Bangladesh	
1975-90	South Africa	
1979	Iran	
1979-89		Afghanistan
1980-89	Poland	
1984-87		Nicaragua
1986	Philippines	
1987	Argentina	
1989	East Germany	Panama
	Hungary	
	Czechoslovakia	
	Chile	
	Bulgaria	
1991	Estonia	
	Latvia	
	Lithuania	
1991-96		Yugoslavia
2001		Afghanistan
2003		Iraq
2004	Ukraine	
2006	Northern Ireland	

The eighteen nonviolent changes of regime have survived, not without troubles, of course, and nearly all of the countries involved are now free and more or less democratic. The eleven violent changes of regime (eight of which were initiated by the United States) have all led to deeply troubled, violent, undemocratic, and unstable regimes.

Nonviolence is the superior force in the contemporary world. The imagination quails at the horrors which would have resulted if the regime change in South Africa had been accomplished by violence, or if the American civil rights movement of the 1960s hadn't been led largely by trained and committed students of nonviolence. The Middle East, and the West's relations with Islamic countries, would be much better and safer if the Palestinians had resorted to nonviolent means of protest against the Israeli occupation of their land with consistency and perseverance.

Active nonviolent resistance or protest isn't required of all of us. What is required is the continual effort to reject violent revenge or retaliation as an available response to violence of any kind, as well as a growing sensitivity and aversion to the violence which is constantly present in our news and in our entertainment. Active nonviolent resistance is a heroic virtue to which some are called. It must be prepared for with study and training. There's a substantial body of literature on nonviolence theory and nonviolent training, and there's now even a video game, *A Force More Powerful,* which trains the player in nonviolent protest techniques. But most of all, nonviolence requires courage. Gandhi put it this way:

> My creed of nonviolence is an extremely active force. It has no room for cowardice or even weakness. There is hope for a violent man to be some day nonviolent, but there is none for a coward. I have therefore said more than once in these pages that if we do not know how to defend ourselves, our women and our places of worship by the force of suffering, i.e., nonviolence, we must, if we are men, be at least able to defend all these by fighting.

One particularly difficult problem Americans have with understanding and accepting nonviolence is the dominance within American culture of what Walter Wink calls *The Myth of Redemptive Violence.* The myth features a hero, a good ordinary non-reflective person, except (in some cases) for his super-powers, and a villain, who's absolutely evil, usually deformed, monstrous or alien, but often very bright, in a warped sort of way. For the first three-quarters of each story or episode, the hero suffers under, and the common people are abused by, the villain, until the hero is hopelessly trapped. The hero is outside the law and desires revenge. In the last quarter, the hero breaks free, summons his powers, and vanquishes the villain with violence or with extreme violence. This arch-villain is then exiled but usually lives to reappear in another episode. This is the plot of every television cartoon and of every action movie: Superman, Batman, the Lone Ranger, Popeye, James Bond, Jason Bourne, Spiderman, and so on.

As Wink observes, "The myth of redemptive violence is the simplest, laziest, most exciting, uncomplicated, irrational, and primitive depiction of evil the world has ever known." And it's enormously pervasive, in television shows, cartoons, video games, movies, and paperback thrillers. Its simple lessons are that bad guys are other, different, and alien from us, that our heroes who oppose them are above the law, and that violence is good and makes us safe. It takes great effort to unlearn these false lessons; we must begin by seeing these underlying falsehoods in most of our popular entertainment.

A second particular handicap for Americans is the huge war machine of the U.S. Department of Defense. The political power of the Defense Department is so great that it's the only branch of government in the United States which nearly always gets more money each year than the year before, whether external military threats to the United States have increased or decreased. No military expansion ever seems to end. Do we still need troops in Germany? in Japan? Do we need anti-ballistic missiles in Poland? Do we need an F-22 fighter plane, or an F-35 joint strike fighter, when no other power on earth can match the F-15?

The Department of Defense is apparently above the law, as its practice of holding prisoners of war indefinitely, without trial, without the rights of the Geneva Conventions, without habeas corpus, and subject to torture, indicates. For many Americans, however, even well-meant criticism of our military forces is considered unpatriotic, or even treasonous. Our war power is even a kind of religion. We religiously celebrate the armed might of the nation on Memorial Day, Flag Day, Veterans Day, and at every major-league sporting event.

What can a small Christian group do to change this part of American culture? Study the problem itself and the alternative of nonviolence. Mobilize opposition if and when the national government proposes yet another war of choice. Become more conscious of the myth of redemptive violence in our popular culture, and counter its influence if and when we can. And work on energy conservation and the development of renewable sources of energy so that the nation will no longer be tempted to go to war in the Middle East to preserve our access to its oil.

Humility. The fourth commandment is *Act as a humble servant toward all others.*

We live in a historically conscious and culturally conscious age. This means that we understand that our ways of seeing things are deeply affected by our own history and our own culture. We see things differently from the way Islamic Arabs, or Han Chinese, see them. This isn't to say that there are no universal truths, or that we can't know them, but only that our own particular grasp of truth is always historically and culturally conditioned and that it takes great effort and empathy to grasp the way similar truths are expressed in different words and different contexts by those of other cultures or other times.

We Americans are wanting in knowledge of the different languages and different cultures of the world, and this handicaps our nation in dealing with peoples and nations we know little about. At the height of the Iraq occupation, the United States had over a thousand officials and employees at the new American Embassy in the Green Zone in Baghdad, of whom only six were fluent in Arabic. There are more musicians in our armed forces military bands than there are foreign service officers in the United States Foreign Service, and the Foreign Service's budget has been cut.

Are American citizens humbled by this relative ignorance, by the fact that the United States is simply not qualified to do nation-building or to deal responsibly with other nations and cultures? Very few. The attitude of the general public is one of arrogance: we aren't simply on balance a fairly good and fairly successful nation; we're Number One, we're the best. This attitude is found in responsible officials and seen in our dealings with other nations, not least in Iraq.

Is there a problem here to which the commandment of Jesus to be a humble servant to others should apply? I think so. The United States is justly seen by the rest of the world as too powerful and too arrogant. It's difficult to work with allies who see us as too proud to admit our mistakes and our incapacities. Many Americans believe we can export freedom and democracy, and some believe we have a mission to do so. But are we qualified?

The United States has an imperfect government of representative democracy. We've built it by work extending over many centuries, back to the Magna Carta (1215) and before. We have frequent elections, but that isn't all, or even the most important part, of democracy. Three factors – our centuries-old custom and practice of resolving disputes by law rather than by force; our laws which establish civil rights, as interpreted and determined by an independent judicial system; and our relative freedom from corruption in government – are all more fundamental to our democracy than elections. The notion that we can export these traditions, customs, and practices by force of arms is juvenile as well as dangerous. Humble service, not arrogance or righteousness, is required in international relations, and this is what Jesus counseled us to do.

Are there good secular arguments for making humble service, rather than righteousness, our guide in relations with foreign peoples and nations? Of course. In his recent memoir, *Once Upon a Country*, Sari Nusseibeh wrote of the British rulers of Palestine after the first World War, "They also did something that would be repeated innumerable times in the future: they sent in clueless 'experts' to find a solution." The United States did this in Iraq, to our shame and consternation. We mustn't do it again. Refusing to speak to representatives of nations with which we have differences is a good way to avoid finding out if there is common ground on which we can negotiate and agree. We can do better. Calling any person or any nation an "enemy" when we know little or nothing about that person's or that nation's history and culture is foolish. It builds foreign relations on pillars of ignorance and arrogance.

What can a small Christian group do? One way to address the situation is to learn about the history and cultures of other nations and people. Another is to support politicians and officials who advocate a realistic foreign policy and humble and helpful relations with other peoples and other cultures. Another is to get to know your neighbors from other lands. If you know them personally, and know their history, you will know them as persons, not as occupants of pigeonholes. And have your children or grandchildren learn a foreign language if they have the opportunity to do so.

Detachment from Possessions. We arrive at the fifth commandment of Jesus, *Detach yourself from possessions.*

In the United States, about fifty million people are without health insurance of any kind, and millions more are insured under plans with unaffordably high deductible or co-pay provisions. Most of the developed nations of the world adopted one form or another of universal health care systems more than sixty years ago. The United States has long been the only advanced society without some form of universal health care.

Need for health care is unpredictable, and varies widely from person to person. An uninsured illness or injury can easily devastate a family's financial security, and often leads to bankruptcy. The two principal causes of foreclosure on a family's home are loss of a job and an uninsured serious illness. Most health insurance for those under 65 in the United States is provided by private insurers, which compete with each other, and which can retain market share and make money only by adverse selection, that is, by excluding from their insurance pool those with chronic illnesses or adverse risk factors, and by denying coverage for claims whenever possible. This means that the very entities which provide health insurance are incentivized by the market to make coverage unavailable, or to deny coverage for claims as they occur, for those who need it most. Meanwhile, the United States has a national health care insurance system for those over 65 and another for veterans, both of which work reasonably well.

Does this involve any of the commandments of Jesus? It seems to me that the commandment to detach ourselves from possessions applies because the underlying failure to care for the sick is founded in acquisitiveness. Initially, but not as much now, the opposition to universal health care came from medical doctors, who feared that "socialized medicine" would reduce their incomes. More recently, the strongest opposition comes from the insurance companies themselves, as they would lose their profitable businesses. Voters who themselves have employer-provided health insurance have generally not supported those who would require that their good fortune be shared with the less fortunate at public cost. We haven't sufficiently detached ourselves from our possessions. In the parable of the Last Judgment, Jesus spoke directly about this:

> Come, you that are blessed by my Father, inherit the kingdom prepared for you from the foundation of the world; for . . . I was sick and you took care of me . . . . Truly I tell you, just as you did it to one of the least of the members of my family, you did it to me. (Mt 25:34,36,40)

Are there good secular policy reasons for adopting national universal health care? There are. We can't as a nation continue to allow so many millions to live outside our health insurance systems. This forces them, most of whom can't afford private health care insurance, to forego or delay diagnosis and treatment of their ills until the illness or injury becomes much more expensive to treat, or, worse yet, becomes untreatable. We can't continue to devote 20% of each health care dollar, some 300 billion dollars annually, to adverse selection, claims denial, sales efforts, and private profit.

What can a small Christian group do? Many good people volunteer in hospitals, nursing homes, and free clinics for the care of the poor and ill. The major step to be taken, perhaps in the current administration, is for the United States to join the rest of the world's advanced nations and adopt one form or another of universal health care insurance.

We've completed our review of the five commandments of Jesus as they apply to public life. I suggest that, taken as a whole, the five commandments form the basis for accurate diagnosis of our most severe social problems. Once correctly diagnosed, the problems can be treated with realistic and sound local, national, and foreign policy reforms. It's clearly the better policy to refrain from deciding that others, outsiders, are our enemies, and that we can't talk to them. It's more prudent to engage those whose friendship is doubtful with respect, honesty, and circumspection. It's practical and prudent to forgive past wrongs and go forward. We need intelligent and sensitive reform of our immigration laws. Retaliation and revenge are counter-productive bases for policies, as well as immoral ones. Military violence is no longer a useful instrument of policy. America's military force has done more harm than good in all its engagements in the last fifty years. If we wish to encourage democracy, civil liberties, and the rule of law throughout the world, we must be a light to the world, not a fire. There are good practical reasons to provide health insurance to everyone in America.

* * * * *

Now that we've explored and discussed the central ethical teachings of Jesus, can we stop at this point? If you're with me so far, you see that we've found in Jesus a brilliant ethical thinker, and in his five commandments a simple but deep and difficult set of ethical directions. Can we simply accept the ethical teachings of Jesus as worthy to be put into practice in our own private and public lives and skip the theology and religion? An argument can be made for doing so. Jesus himself said, in several different ways, that it's much more important to accept and practice his commandments than it is to recognize him as savior. "Not everyone who says to me, 'Lord, Lord,' will enter the kingdom of heaven, but only the one who does the will of my Father in heaven" (Mt 7:21).

Jesus was quite clear about his ethical teachings. He was less clear about the precise nature of his own relationship to God, or about the doctrine of the Trinity, and virtually silent about the constitution of the church, although these doctrinal questions have received much more attention from Christian leaders, scholars, and teachers throughout history than his ethical teachings. If we adopt and follow the central ethical injunctions of Jesus in our own lives and take no view on matters of doctrine, we are certainly followers of Jesus and full participants in establishing the kingdom of God in our own lives and in the world. If, therefore, some of us are persuaded to follow the five commandments of Jesus but are not ready to believe the central doctrines of the Christian churches, that's a reasonable and good position to hold.

History and experience teach us, however, that assent to a set of ethical teachings is usually not enough. Great movements are not led by philosophers. They're led by leaders whose personal example, attractiveness, and charisma inspire a personal devotion and loyalty to the ideas and ideals of the leader. For example, consider utilitarianism. In nineteenth century England, some fine ethical philosophers, Jeremy Bentham, James Mill, John Stuart Mill, and others, described and advocated a highly reasonable and attractive set of ethical principles, called utilitarianism, which enjoys favor among ethical philosophers to the present day. But utilitarianism lacked an exemplary leader and a cause and has remained an academic ethical system.

In contrast, Jesus was more than a brilliant ethical philosopher, more than a scholar with a deep understanding of evolutionary psychology and cultural anthropology. He spoke authoritatively about religious practices, about God, and about his unique role as God's representative on earth. He preached the inauguration of God's kingdom on earth and promised eternal life to those who followed him. There's strong evidence that he could and did work healing miracles, and equally strong evidence that he himself rose to a new life after his death. He taught not only by word but by the example of his life and death, and he called his followers to imitate him. He is the center and founder of one of the world's great religions. That's why who and what he is really matters.

The followers of Jesus identified him as divine as well as human. The nature of the Father of whom Jesus spoke, and the way in which Jesus was both divine and human, have been and are central teachings of all Christian churches from the earliest days of Christianity. We need to understand these teachings in a way which makes them coherent and credible for our time if we are to make the personal commitment to Jesus for which he asked, a commitment upon which our assent and commitment to his five commandments would then be based. So we turn now to examine these central teachings.

Notes and Sources for Further Reading

Barack Obama's speech to the Sojourners/Call to Renewal conference can be found at http://www.sojo.net/index.cfm?action.

The statistics on world prison confinement are from the World Prison Population List (fourth edition, 2003) of the United Kingdom Home Office, at publications.rds@homeoffice.gsi.gov.uk. Similar and updated statistics are in an article in the New York Times, April 23, 2008, p. 1.

Descriptions and analysis of WWII bombings are found in James Carroll's *House of War: The Pentagon and the Disastrous Rise of American Power* (Houghton Mifflin, 2006), pp. 40-102.

The computer game, *A Force More Powerful*, can be found at www.aforcemorepowerful.org/game/.

I found the quotation from Gandhi in his *All Men Are Brothers* (Continuum, 1980), p. 97.

Walter Wink's description of the myth of redemptive violence is found in his *Engaging the Powers* (Fortress Press, 1992), pp. 13-31. The quotation is from p. 22.

The quotation from Sari Nusseibeh is from his *Once Upon a Country* (Farrar, Straus & Giroux, 2007), p. 32.

Utilitarianism is explained and defended by Robert Wright in his *The Moral Animal* (Vintage Books, 1994), pp. 327-44.

IX

THE CHRISTIAN DOCTRINES OF GOD AND JESUS

"The Father is in me and I am in the Father." (Jn 10:38)

THIS ISN'T A BOOK about Christian theology and dogma; it's a book about the five commandments of Jesus. But for most of us, a practical commitment to follow the five commandments will come only with a personal commitment to Jesus as leader, teacher, redeemer, and unique mediator of God's will. To make this kind of personal commitment to Jesus, we need to know something about just who and what he was, human, or divine, or both, and to have some understanding of his special relationship with the Father. And to understand his relationship with his Father, we need to know something about the nature of God and the meaning of the Trinity.

The traditional teachings of the Christian churches don't make this easy. Traditional religious art doesn't help. If you've spent some time in an art museum, you may be forgiven for having the impression that God is a committee of three: a gloomy-looking old man with a long white beard, a pious-looking young man with a short brown beard, and a dove. We have to be careful that these pictures don't interfere with our thinking about God and Jesus. The doctrine of the Trinity doesn't clear this up. There are three persons in God. The Father is God. The Son is God. The Holy Spirit is God. There is only one God.

The doctrine of Jesus is equally mysterious. Jesus is truly a man. Jesus is truly God. There is only one Jesus. How can this be? Many people throw up their hands and don't think about it much. In James Joyce's *Ulysses*, Buck Mulligan throws up his hands and sings the ballad of Joking Jesus, the first stanza of which is

> I'm the queerest young fellow that ever you heard.
> My mother's a jew, my father's a bird.
> With Joseph the joiner I cannot agree,
> So here's to disciples and Calvary.

So I conclude that, to understand and to accept the commitment required by Jesus both to himself and to his five commandments, we need to reexamine Christianity's foundational doctrines.

The foundational Christian doctrines are the existence and benevolence of God, the relationship of Jesus of Nazareth to God which makes him in some way divine, and the doctrine of the Trinity. In their traditional formulations, as for example in the Nicene Creed, where Jesus is said to be "begotten, not made, of one substance with the Father," these doctrines can be quite difficult for modern educated people to understand, let alone believe. In part this is due to the fact that the doctrines are often (as here) expressed in an archaic philosophical language, and in forms which responded to questions raised in the fourth and fifth centuries but have little or nothing to say in response to questions of modern times. One result of this is that the traditional formulations hinder rather than help our understanding of the redemptive or saving activities of Jesus, the part played by his five commandments, and our part in these activities.

Some very good modern Christian theologians have thought in depth about these foundational doctrines and have reinterpreted them for our times. What follows is my own statement of what I've learned from their interpretations.

When we consider the Christian teachings about God, about the relationship of Jesus to God, and about the Trinity, we're dealing with matters which are known by faith. So I begin by describing how I understand faith.

Every person has unspoken, even inarticulate, views on life's fundamental questions: Is life worth living? Do we have a purpose and a goal? Is the real world generally benign or malevolent? Is there a right way to live? Can we find out what it is? Is love for others ultimately a good thing? Is there a higher being? Is he or she benevolent, indifferent, or hostile to us? We form our own answers to these questions, even if the answers are provisional and subject to change, in order to live mature lives. None of these questions is answerable the way scientific or historical questions are answered, by studying data, observing events, and reasoning toward a conclusion. Thinking clearly helps; study, experience, and tradition help; but we must choose. And we each choose a set of working answers to the fundamental questions in a partially pre-logical, pre-verbal way, forming a set of rational but also gut-level choices and decisions. And then we live by the answers we have chosen; we make and keep commitments based on these answers. This is faith.

Note that faith is the response to fundamental and mostly transcendental questions: that is, questions having to do with God or with our personal meaning and value systems. Faith is not the response to questions to which the answers depend on empirical evidence. For example, I know that Jesus was a first-century Jewish teacher, that he taught his five commandments, and that he was crucified by the Romans in Jerusalem from the historical data, not as a matter of faith. Whether, how, to what extent, and in what way Jesus is divine is a matter for faith, because it has to do with God.

Note also that a nonbeliever also has a faith, a provisional set of answers to life's fundamental questions, a personal meaning and value system, which he or she lives by. The content may be different, but it's still faith, because both believers and nonbelievers must formulate their own personal sets of answers to these questions to get on with life.

Beliefs, as I use the term, are something different from faith. Beliefs are propositions expressing, symbolizing, or defining the objects of our faith, our answers to the fundamental questions, so that they can be communicated to others. An example of a set of belief statements is the Nicene Creed, a fourth century statement of Christian beliefs, said as a prayer in many Christian church services. As there can be several ways of stating a truth, there can be several different belief statements about a single object of faith. Belief statements can change while the object of faith remains the same. Sometimes belief statements must be changed, simply to retain their original meanings, as languages and the meanings of words change over time.

Two of the fundamental, gut-level questions to which faith is directed are: Is there a God? And is God benevolent to us? The answers matter, because the answers affect the answers to all the rest of the fundamental questions. They're hard questions for a number of reasons. There's no unambiguously direct evidence for the existence and presence of an all-knowing, all-powerful spiritual being. It's very difficult or impossible to imagine God without just imagining an all-powerful human, with or without a long white beard. The logical arguments, or "proofs," for the existence of God don't satisfy and are too much argued over. And so many unpleasant people have told us what God wants, or how God will act toward us if we don't change our ways, or have described God as an interfering and demanding person, that some of us resist the idea of God as an object of a faith commitment.

The German theologian Friedrich Schleiermacher, who taught in Berlin in the early nineteenth century, is the first and one of the greatest of modern Christian theologians. He begins his major theological work, *The Christian Faith*, by observing that at a fundamental level in our conscious life, there is in each of us both a consciousness of being dependent upon other persons and things for what we are and what we have, and a consciousness that some people and some things are dependent upon us. He then observes that there is also in each of us a consciousness of absolute dependence upon some being, which itself is dependent upon nothing else and is absolutely free. Finally, he observes that, from our general experience, we discover that many other people also feel likewise absolutely dependent on something or someone outside themselves. The being upon whom we're all absolutely dependent we call God. Schleiermacher calls this consciousness of God's existence and of our dependence on God our "God-consciousness."

This may seem terribly abstract. You may not have experienced in your own mind a consciousness of absolute dependence on a higher power. In his *The Varieties of Religious Experience*, the eminent American psychologist and philosopher William James studied religious experiences in his capacity as a psychologist and quoted extensively from the descriptions by other writers of their own mystical experiences. Most of the narrators whom James quotes are describing events in which their God-consciousnesses were open to the presence of, and had an experience of, a higher power. James, a scientist, a skeptic, and a pragmatist, finds that these experiences are uniformly pre-verbal. The descriptions of them, in each narrator's traditional religious language, tell us nothing about religious doctrine. James concludes, however, that substantially all the narrators were, at the time of their experiences, in touch in some way with a real higher power, a higher power that had a real effect on the life of the person experiencing the communication. James sums up his study of these experiences this way:

> The further limits of our being plunge, it seems to me, into an altogether other dimension of existence from the sensible and merely "understandable" world. Name it the mystical region, or the supernatural region, whichever you choose. So far as our ideal impulses originate in this region

(and most of them do originate in it, for we find them possessing us in a way for which we cannot articulately account), we belong to it in a more intimate sense than that in which we belong to the visible world, for we belong in the most intimate sense wherever our ideals belong. *Yet the unseen region in question is not merely ideal, for it produces effects in this world.* When we commune with it, work is actually done upon our finite personality, for we are turned into new men, and consequences in the way of conduct follow in the natural world upon our regenerative change. But that which produces effects within another reality must be termed a reality itself, so I feel as if we had no philosophic excuse for calling the unseen or mystical world unreal.

God is the natural appellation, for us Christians at least, for the supreme reality, so I will call this higher part of the universe by the name of God. We and God have business with each other; and in opening ourselves to his influence our deepest destiny is fulfilled.

In effect, James has collected and presented evidence that God-consciousness exists in many persons as a real connection with a real God.

In this light, the classic "proofs" for the existence of God can probably be better understood as ways of directing our attention to interior reflections in which we can perceive our absolute dependence on a being which itself is absolutely independent. Thus, for example, we reflect that we, and everything else in known creation, exist, but at one time did not exist; and we, and everything else, change, and are not now what we or they once were or will be. But if everything is contingent and changing, why is there anything? One answer is that there is a being which always exists and doesn't ever change, and upon which all other beings are dependent. I don't know if there's another satisfactory answer. This reflection puts us in touch with the concept of our absolute dependence, and thus perhaps in touch with our innate God-consciousness.

Methods of meditation and contemplation, both Christian and non-Christian, have been used for ages by men and women, in many cases with great effect, to place themselves in touch with their innate God-consciousness. Diligent practice of one or another of these methods is a valuable and important way for many of us to deepen our spirituality and anchor ourselves against the cares, distractions, and troubles of life in this world.

For some serious writers on this subject, their particular consciousness of God is expressed as an insight or intuition based on our innate awareness of moral rules.   In many situations we find we have an intuitive sense of what is right and what is wrong, apart from and preceding any feeling or judgment about what is useful or practical or what is required by our laws or our culture.   This intuition, or gut feeling, which we find we share with all normal human beings, yet which seems to come from outside ourselves, is an indication to many that there is an absolute being who is the source of our innate knowledge of right and wrong, whom we call God.   This evidence for God is powerfully and persuasively explained and defended by John Henry Newman in his *A Grammar of Assent* and by C. S. Lewis in his *Mere Christianity*.   Lewis's formulation is adopted by Francis Collins in his recent *The Language of God*.

From this understanding of a higher being upon whom all creation is dependent, we can build up the idea of God very slowly and carefully and appreciate how strange God is, and how difficult it is to imagine her.   Let us start with a being who always exists, who never changes, and upon whom all other beings are absolutely dependent, not only for their creation, but also for their continued existence from moment to moment.   If all things are so dependent on God, and none of them limit her, she is all-powerful.   As God has all powers, she has the power of knowledge in full, and she is all-knowing.   As God's power extends at every moment to everything she has created and sustains in being, she is omnipresent.   As God never changes, as change would imply attaining a power or perfection she didn't have before, or losing one she had, she is eternal.   This means God is outside of time, for time is simply the measure of change.

Let's take this bit about being eternal slowly; it turns out to be very important.   When I reflect on my own life, I'm conscious that my life and my being is never completely possessed by me all at once, but in parts which precede and follow one another.   This is true of all of us and of all we know.   Time is change, or the measure of change.   I'm not now the person I once was, nor am I the person I'll be tomorrow.   Time is a fundamental limitation upon our possession of our existence.   Time does not limit God.   Woody Allen once said that "Time is nature's way of keeping everything from happening at once."   With God, everything does happen at once.   God herself is perfect and does not change. Time has no meaning for God. This isn't altered by God's creation of a universe which changes and which does exist in time. God remains outside of time.

This concept is so counter-intuitive that we need to consider it more closely or we'll instinctively and erroneously place God back into time. Imagination can be misleading, but I find some help in imagining the time line of the universe projected onto a very large semicircular movie screen, with God as the audience (and producer and director too) watching the whole show at once. God can see all that was and all that is and all that will be at the same time because it's all on the screen (his screen) at the same time. God is completely present at any point in time in the life of the universe, but God isn't thereby limited to that point in time. Since God can see the whole screen at once, he's fully present at all times at all points in the universe's time line without being a part of time. It follows that God doesn't have a memory, nor does he have prescience, or knowledge of the future as future. God doesn't foresee what is to happen, and he can't change his mind. God has only "now," and everything is "now" to God.

While I accept this reasoning, and this conception of God, I can't imagine what it's like to know things the way God knows them. God knows my whole life, and yours, all at once. She doesn't turn her attention first to one person, then to another; she sees them both now. God doesn't think discursively, one thing after another; she doesn't remember; she doesn't forget. As we can only think about God or talk about her in human language, with human ideas, our thoughts and our talk about God are always anthropomorphic. God isn't pleased with our good actions, nor displeased with our bad ones; she doesn't react or change because of what we do. Who can say what is God's will, what she wants?

That God is all-powerful is clear. Without some word from God about it, it would not be clear (to me at least) that God is benevolent toward humans. The Hebrew Scriptures present an inconsistent God, very much like a stubborn old man, whose attitude toward humanity keeps changing. At one time he creates the earth, and men and women, and sees that it is good; some time later he changes his mind and kills all humans except Noah and his family. The teaching of Jesus on this point is new and clear: God cares for us as a good father cares for his children, and he loves us. This is good news. It's certainly one of the most welcoming and attractive teachings of Christianity.

So, putting all of the above together, and adding the teachings of Jesus, my own life experience, and the elements of my own personality, I find I believe, on a very fundamental or gut level, in the existence of a benevolent and loving God. I'm not a mystic. The closest I've ever come to a mystical experience is the exalting feeling of performing one of the great religious choral works: the Bach *B Minor Mass,* the Brahms *German Requiem*, the Berlioz *Requiem*, and others. My God-consciousness isn't well developed.

I have a personal confession to make: I have a problem with the commandment to love God with my whole heart, and so forth. Love, to me, is what I have for my wife, my children, my family and my friends. I extend that feeling, somewhat attenuated, to my neighbors, to my fellow Americans, and to all the people in the world. It's bound up with a wish and desire that things go well with the ones I love, that they may have peace and happiness rather than pains and suffering, that they may have a good life. How can I feel that way toward God, when I've no idea what peace and happiness, or a good life, can be for God, and when, if there are such things in his existence, he has them in fullness already?

Respect, yes; respect, even awe, for God's power and his wisdom (which I can't understand). Gratitude, yes; for bringing me and those I love into being and sustaining us in being, for creating a world in which we can live, and for giving us such abilities and opportunities as we've been given. Obedience to his commandments, yes; I believe that God has, through Jesus, and through the Christian churches, given us good advice as to what kind of conduct leads to a good life, an improved world, and (one hopes) an everlasting reward, and that it would be quite imprudent not to try as best we can to live by this counsel as we understand it. Worship, I don't know; God doesn't need me to sing him hymns of praise. Perhaps it's a good thing for me to be reminded of his power, his wisdom, and his benevolence at regular intervals and at regular times, at Sunday worship services. Perhaps my participation helps others who also take part. Love, I don't know. I hope that respect, gratitude, and obedience, taken together, add up to the love of God which is enjoined by the commandment. I suppose that if God really loves me, they do. And I'm happy that the first epistle of John instructs us, "Beloved, since God loved us so much, we ought also to love one another" (1 Jn 4:11).

God is not only almost impossible to understand; he also seems to be very remote. For the most part, he seems to let us alone. When humans cry for help, he very rarely responds in any recognizable way. We're susceptible to fooling ourselves about God. When someone says that God has told him or her this or that, I don't argue with him or her, but I don't believe it. I make only one exception, for Jesus. Not for the writers of Scripture; they were historians, teachers, and in the case of many of the Hebrew Scripture writers, mythmakers. In general, God doesn't intervene in natural human life, and she has rarely told us what she wants us to do. She generally leaves it to us to figure it out for ourselves.

Jesus is the singular exception. He was recognized as a singular exception during his life and after his death by many who knew him directly. It's an act of faith, or a judgment of faith, to believe that God authorized and directed Jesus to speak for him to the human race, because every judgment or belief about God is an act of faith. It is, in my view, a reasonable (though not "provable") judgment to make, based on all the facts and circumstances. Consider the principal historical facts:

1. the profound insight which Jesus had into the human condition, and his teachings which addressed this condition so directly;
2. his extraordinary command of teaching techniques, illustration, metaphor, and parable;
3. his blameless and exemplary life;
4. his claims to know important facts about the nature of God, the destiny of humans, and his own unique role as mediator between God and humans, claims which, if not true, would be very difficult to reconcile with the rest of what we know about his character and his intelligence;
5. the strong historical tradition that he worked many miracles in the name of God;
6. his exemplary death;
7. the strong evidence that he rose from the dead and appeared many times to many of his disciples; and

8.   the dramatic and otherwise inexplicable change in his
     followers after he was gone.

That Jesus was a true and unique messenger from God to humans
isn't a difficult conclusion to reach. But soon after his resurrection,
early Christians proclaimed him to be divine, and the Christian
churches have done so ever since. The Christian churches have also
been unswervingly monotheistic. Well, there were some swerves, with
among others the gnostics, Origen, and the Arians; but all the explanations of Jesus as a separate and lesser deity were repudiated by the
Christian church in its first few centuries. So proclaiming Jesus as
divine has always raised as many questions as answers.

At the outset of a discussion of whether Jesus was divine, or
human, or both, and if both, how can this be possible, is the question
whether or not it makes a practical difference. It isn't immediately
apparent that it does. That is, the belief statement that Jesus is truly
God may not affect our commitment to him or influence our actions;
it may be a belief statement but not an object of faith, which implies
commitment. From what Jesus said, we know that he wanted his
followers to observe his ethical teachings, particularly his five commandments, as the true word of God, to accept his teachings about
God and about the rewards promised to those who follow his
teachings, and to put their trust in him personally. Jesus was clear
about these; he could be quite clear when he wanted to be.

But Jesus was far from clear about his precise relationship to God,
or whether he was the Son of God, and what that might mean. He
clearly wanted to be understood and accepted as a unique and trustworthy messenger from God and as the mediator between God and
humanity. Once one accepts Jesus as true messenger and mediator, the
only reasonable way to put this acceptance into practice is to undertake
and persevere in the practice of the rules of conduct he taught. In this
light, the precise nature of his relationship to God doesn't seem to
matter very much.

But it mattered a lot to the early Christian church, and after much
debate and mutual excommunication of opposing theologians, the
Christian church decided first, at the council of Nicaea in 325, that the
"Word" that was incarnate in Jesus was of the same nature as God and
thus truly divine, and then, at the council of Chalcedon in 451, that
Jesus is truly God and truly human. We need to examine this latter

conclusion carefully because it's so central to the Christian tradition, both because one simply can't explain Christianity without dealing with this question, whether our own generation thinks that it's important or not, and also because misunderstanding the nature of Jesus can cloud and obscure our understanding of his role and ours in God's plan for humanity.

The philosophical and theological reasoning leading to the Chalcedonian doctrine was worked out by Greek theologians of the fourth and fifth centuries. Two important things follow from the fact that these theologians were (for the most part) fourth and fifth century Greeks:

First, many Greek theologians seemed to think that the gap (or chasm) between God and humans could only be bridged and salvation made possible by an event which created a blood relationship, a kind of intermarriage, between God and humans. That is to say, God became human so that we humans could become divine, which is what they thought it is to be saved. This is the real reason for the importance in Christian tradition of the virgin birth of Jesus. God, as Spirit, was directly the father, and Mary, the virgin, was the mother, of a child born of intermarriage between God and a human person. Classical Greek and Roman mythology, with its countless stories of procreation between gods and humans, may well have influenced this way of thinking.

Second, the Greek theologians were neo-Platonists, a school of philosophy which included in its basic terms concepts such as "person" and "nature," and "spirit" and "matter," which were difficult to grasp at that time and are almost impenetrable to understanding in the modern world, which uses the same words for entirely different concepts.

The traditional Chalcedonian doctrine about Jesus, which is still a central Christian doctrine, is that he is one "person" who has two "natures," one a divine "nature," making him the second "person" in the Trinity, and one a human "nature," making him a human being. This doctrine, when examined closely, seems to contain some insoluble problems:

First, we can't conceive of a real "person," an individual self-identity or constant unity of conscious life, which is neither human nor divine, but which can become either (or both) depending on whether it unites with a human set of powers, attributes, and qualities or a divine set of powers, attributes, and qualities. I don't "have" a human nature; I'm a genetically unique human being. "Human nature" simply describes the fact that I'm very much like you or like any other person. My "personhood" is human. I have no personhood, no continuing conscious self-identity, apart from being a human being. So if Jesus was truly human, he was a human person. He was not a floating person, neither human nor divine, but capable of becoming either by uniting with either a human or a divine nature, because there is no such thing.

Second, if Jesus was both divine and human, did he have both a divine will and a human will? If he had one will, was it divine, in which case his humanity was incomplete, or was it human, in which case his divine nature was incomplete? If Jesus had two wills, wouldn't there be two persons, two independent continuing conscious self-identities, even if the two wills always agreed? What Jesus said about this was, "I have come from heaven, not to do my own will, but to do the will of the one who sent me" (Jn 6:38). If this means anything, it means that Jesus had a human will, and God the Father had a different will, which Jesus didn't call "my own." Similarly, if Jesus had two intellects, one a human intellect, which sees things one at a time and proceeds from one thing to another, and the other a divine intellect, which sees and understands all things all at once and doesn't change, how could these have coexisted in the same person, without the divine intellect wholly blotting out the human?

What actually happens in the mind of the traditional Christian believer is that we accept the formula of "one person with two natures" and don't examine it. We think of Jesus as God the Son, the Second Person of the Trinity, who after being in heaven for a long time comes down to earth and takes on human form in the person of Jesus. We then find it very difficult to understand Jesus as a real human being. I find this way of thinking about Jesus hard to distinguish from the stories in Greek mythology or in Ovid's *Metamorphoses* where gods often took on human or animal form when they came down from Olympus to deal with ordinary humans, or from the science fiction stories, like the *X-Files*, in which an alien takes on the appearance of a human being.

But it's traditional Christian doctrine that Jesus is truly human as well as truly divine. If we lose sight of his genuine humanity, we won't see him as an example, or understand his mission, or feel the attraction of the call to imitate him. If we don't believe that Jesus is a real human person, like ourselves, we won't really believe that his example can be followed by real human people like ourselves. It isn't enough simply to assert, as the Nicene Creed does, that the Son of God, begotten of the Father before all ages, became man and was truly man. This leads to the confusions and contradictions described above. Some Christian theologians have tried to deal with this problem by teaching that the divine attributes of Jesus were hidden, or became "quiescent," during the life of Jesus. But this simply leads us back to the notion of a god in metamorphosis, a god in disguise, a deceptive god. We need a point of departure different from that of classical Christian theology to understand Jesus.

The better way to describe the relationship of Jesus to God is to start from what we know and then work from what Jesus said about himself. What we know is that Jesus of Nazareth was a real human being, a young man of Jewish descent and upbringing, who preached in Galilee, Judea, and neighboring places, and who was executed in Jerusalem in the early first century. What Jesus said about himself and about his relationship with God is contained in many of his sayings, mostly recorded in the Gospel of John. Here are some of them:

> I came from God and now I am here. I did not come on my own, but he sent me. (Jn 8:42)

> If you loved me, you would rejoice that I am going to the Father, because the Father is greater than I. (Jn 14:28)

> The works that my Father has given me to complete, the very works that I am doing, testify on my behalf that the Father has sent me. (Jn 5:36)

> I can do nothing on my own. As I hear, I judge; and my judgment is just, because I seek to do not my own will, but the will of him who sent me. (Jn 5:30)

> I judge no one. Yet even if I do judge, my judgment is valid; for it is not I alone who judge, but I and the Father who sent me. In your law it is written that the testimony of two witnesses is valid. I testify on my own behalf, and the Father who sent me testifies on my behalf. (Jn 8:15-18)

The Son can do nothing on his own, but only what he sees the Father doing; for whatever the Father does, the Son does likewise. The Father loves the Son and shows him all that he himself is doing; and he will show him greater works than these, so that you will be astonished. (Jn 5:19-20)

My food is to do the will of him who sent me and to complete his work. (Jn 4:34)

Everything that the Father gives me will come to me, and anyone who comes to me I will never drive away; for I have come down from heaven, not to do my own will, but the will of him who sent me. And this is the will of him who sent me, that I should lose nothing of all that he has given me, but raise it up on the last day. This is indeed the will of my Father, that all who see the Son and believe in him may have eternal life; and I will raise them up on the last day. (Jn 6:37-40)

Everyone who has heard and learned from the Father comes to me. No one has seen the Father except the one who is from God; he has seen the Father. (Jn 6:45-46)

The Father and I are one. (Jn 10:30)

The Father is in me and I am in the Father. (Jn 10:38)

I am the way, and the truth, and the life. No one comes to the Father except through me. If you know me, you will know my Father also. From now on, you do know him and have seen him. (Jn 14:6-7)

For the most part, as we see, Jesus describes himself as a human person sent by God, whom he always calls the Father. The Father is greater than Jesus. Jesus can do nothing on his own. The Father is a different person. The testimony of Jesus and the separate testimony of the Father, manifest in Jesus's miracles, is the testimony of two different witnesses. Jesus has his own will, a human will, and the Father has a different will, the divine will: "I seek to do not my own will, but the will of him who sent me." Jesus has a direct perception of the Father and what the Father is doing, but in a way which the human mind can receive, in parts and as needed, not in one overwhelming blast of omniscience: "The Father loves the Son and shows him all that he himself is doing; *and he will show him greater works than these* . . . ." Jesus doesn't know everything that God knows. When talking about the last days of the world, Jesus himself said, "But about that day and hour no one knows, neither the angels of heaven, *nor the Son*, but only the Father" (Mt 24:36).

But Jesus also describes his relationship with the Father as unique among all humans for all time: "No one has seen the Father except the one who is from God; he has seen the Father." Jesus alone provides the path, and is the path, by which men may reach God: "I am the way, and the truth, and the life. No one comes to the Father except through me." And Jesus describes this unique relationship between him and his Father as a real union: "The Father is in me and I am in the Father." "The Father and I are one."

There's a balance which we must maintain in talking and thinking about Jesus. We need to understand that he was really a human person with a fully human life and that this human life was not overwhelmed by divine power. But we also need to understand that he wasn't just one of the many holy persons who have received, or who have believed they have received, a special revelation from God, and who have set about teaching and doing good works based on that revelation. Jesus's own sayings show how difficult the balance is; sometimes he speaks of himself as human – "I can do nothing on my own"; and sometimes he speaks of himself as God – "Before Abraham came to be, I am" (Jn 8:58).

Earlier in this chapter I spoke of the God-consciousness we all possess, a consciousness of absolute dependence upon a being which itself is dependent on nothing else, and who is the source of our intuitive knowledge of right and wrong. God-consciousness is a wholly human faculty of receptiveness to God, and it varies widely in intensity and development from one person to another. Friedrich Schleier-macher, who developed this concept of God-consciousness, uses it to describe the unique relationship of Jesus to God. This is his description, in my words, as I understand it.

In Jesus, alone of all humans, this faculty of God-consciousness was full; it was at the maximum level which is compatible with and doesn't destroy real human life; and it was at that level throughout his life. That's the real miracle of the birth of Jesus: Jesus, an ordinary human being, conceived and born in the ordinary human way, was chosen by God and given at birth a consciousness of God essentially identical to, but at a different level of magnitude than, that of any other human. It's as if, for all the rest of us, consciousness is a darkened room which gradually fills with light as we mature, and there is a little aperture, like a camera shutter, in one wall, which opens from time to time, and through which we have a consciousness of God and of his presence, but intermittently, and always as through a glass, darkly. In Jesus, the shutter is wide, clear, and always open, and he always sees God.

Since Jesus's God-consciousness is an expansion of a truly human capacity, it doesn't make Jesus less fully human, although in Jesus, unlike us, the power of his God-consciousness was sufficiently strong that it made him permanently free from sin, from error, and from bad judgment. Jesus recognized this power from the outset as unique to him, and this is the power he described when he said of himself, "No one has seen the Father except the one who is from God; *he has seen the Father.*" This description of the relationship of Jesus to the Father is wholly consistent with what Jesus said about that relationship in the dozen passages from John's Gospel quoted above.

The God-consciousness of Jesus didn't override his human intelligence and his growth as a human personality. The Gospel of Luke records that "Jesus increased in wisdom and in years, and in divine and human favor" (Lk 2:52). Tales of miracles performed by the infant Jesus are told in the apocryphal Gospels, but nowhere in the accepted canonical Scriptures. In all probability they never happened. Jesus didn't know all that God knows in the way which God knows it, because that activity can't be performed by a human intelligence. But he saw all things with his human intelligence and vision, from the earliest moments of life, in the light of his God-consciousness, in the light of the presence of God within him.

In biological terms, Jesus's cerebral cortex, with the guidance of his God-consciousness, was always in control of his limbic system without effort or struggle. This implies that he couldn't do evil and that in a practical sense he couldn't be tempted to do evil. That is to say, a temptation implies a real possibility that the tempted person will give in to the temptation. The God-consciousness of Jesus was so full and so open to God at all times that the possibility that he could ignore his God-consciousness and do evil was never real. Jesus proceeded from innocence to virtue and merit without fault. As he learned about evil and error by living a normal life and by observing and interacting with other people, he became conscious of the fact that he was unique among human beings in his fully-developed God-consciousness and in the powers that accompanied it.

Another way of imagining what this must have been like is to think of Jesus as always hearing the voice of God in his head, teaching him, counseling him, warning him, consoling him. As each of us carries on a sort of interior dialogue with ourselves, more or less continuing throughout our waking hours, so Jesus was able to carry on an interior dialogue with God at all times; and God was really there participating in the dialogue. As Jesus thought like a human, in a discursive, progressive, rational way, which isn't how God knows things, so in a way Jesus was engaged throughout his life in the continuous translation of God's thought and will into human thought and human language. The contemporary English Catholic theologian James Alison expresses this understanding of Jesus in only slightly different language:

> Jesus was able to answer the Sadducees in the way he did because *his* imagination and heart were not darkened, senseless, futile. That is to say, he did not share the condition of the human heart in which, according to St. Paul, we all share. This was not because he was not human, nor because he was God instead of being human, but because *his fully human imagination was capable of being fixed on the ineffable effervescence and vivacity, power and deathlessness of God in a way which seems almost unimaginable to us.*

Jesus's intellectual development took place in the normal human way, but because he had the light of God's presence within him he saw things more clearly and more deeply, and without error. In the only story of Jesus's youth found in the Gospels, he went with his parents to the Passover festival in Jerusalem when he was twelve. After the festival was over, he stayed behind, and after three days he was found with the teachers in the temple, "listening to them and asking them questions. And all who heard him were amazed at his understanding and his answers." When his mother scolded him for staying behind, he answered, "Why were you looking for me? Did you not know that I must be about my Father's business?" (Lk 2:41-51). We see here an exceptionally bright young student of the law and of the Jewish religion, but not a deity in disguise; a twelve-year-old who could get a scolding from his mother; but already someone who called God his Father, which was part of his new and revolutionary way of thinking and teaching about God.

We also see developing in him at an early age his consciousness of his mission. It was his duty to do everything only in the light of his God-consciousness, in the light of the divine will which was present in a unique way within him. As he was faithful and constant in this duty, God acted and operated through him: "I can do nothing on my own. As I hear, I judge; and my judgment is just, because I seek to do not my own will, but the will of him who sent me" (Jn 5:30).

In the sense I've just described, Jesus is truly God and truly man. His human mind, his human will and his human consciousness were filled with the consciousness of God, but they weren't overwhelmed by it. He could and did distinguish between his own will and "the will of him who sent me." But Jesus was fully united at all times with God his Father: "The Father is in me and I am in the Father." "The Father and I are one." In this sense, Jesus is truly God. And if we understand the belief statement, "Jesus is truly God," to mean that Jesus was a real human person, who said what he said and did what he did in the light of a total openness of his consciousness to the one true God, we can understand the object of that belief statement, Jesus, as a human person to whom we can commit ourselves on a gut level. Then it's a belief statement expressing a faith decision and commitment.

Jesus's teachings of his five commandments play a crucial role in leading us to this commitment to him. As we saw at the beginning of this chapter, we each have a personal and fundamental value structure, our personal set of faith decisions we live by. When we are children, we each learn and build for ourselves a childlike and ideal value structure, an ideal moral world where we can experience peace and a non-judging, forgiving, nonviolent, and caring love for all others, whatever their race, nation, or culture. As we progress through adolescence to maturity, we learn that the world treats these ideals as impossible to achieve and impractical to desire. Most of us respond by putting our higher ideals on the shelf and adjusting our personal value structures, that is, our faith, to what the world tells us is possible. But the higher ideals are still there, on the shelf, and we often wish they were practical.

Jesus's teachings of his five commandments allows us and calls us to return the higher ideals of our childhood to our personal value systems, because his teachings tell us that striving for these higher ideals is possible and practical (though difficult). As we realize this, it's like breathing fresh air once again after years in a stuffy room. We add to these teachings of Jesus his teachings that God is our Father, that God is benevolent, loving, caring, and concerned about us, and that living the five commandments of Jesus is God's will and part of God's plan. Then our fundamental meaning and value structures change in a real way. We are then ready to commit ourselves in faith to Jesus, the person whose teachings and example have shown us that our higher ideals can be our practical and realistic goals, and to commit ourselves in fidelity to the practice of his five commandments. This is how faith in Jesus arises and lives in us.

We conclude with a brief discussion of the traditional Christian doctrine of the Trinity: that one God is composed of three persons, the Father, the Son (Jesus), and the Holy Spirit. The historical purpose of the doctrine of the Trinity was to establish that it is the one true God himself, and not some lesser divinity, who is united with human nature first in the person of Jesus and second in the person of the Holy Spirit present with the followers of Jesus. The union of God with Jesus I have just described. The union of God with the followers of Jesus is similar, though without Jesus's unique expansion of God-consciousness. For Christians, God is thus manifest to the world in three ways: in creating and sustaining the world; in the person of Jesus of Nazareth; and in the followers of Jesus. We recognize and bring to mind these three manifestations when we call God in the first manifestation the Father, in the second manifestation the Son, and in the third manifestation the Holy Spirit. Hence many traditional Christian prayers end with the words, "Glory be to the Father, and to the Son, and to the Holy Spirit, as it was in the beginning, is now, and ever shall be, world without end, Amen."

It has always been clear Christian doctrine that there is one God and that all of God's external actions toward the world are acts of the one God, without distinction of persons. That is, the God whom Jesus called "Father" was in reality at all times the Father, the Son, and the Holy Spirit acting together. The Father didn't create the world; God, with her manifestation titles of Father, Son, and Holy Spirit, created the world. Neither the Father nor the Holy Spirit dwelt in Jesus as Son. The one God, Father, Son, and Holy Spirit, dwelt in Jesus and acted in

Jesus through Jesus's expanded God-consciousness. That's why, when Jesus spoke of God's continuing presence with his followers, in sayings which are set forth at the end of Chapter 5, he was never clear whether it would be the Father, the Son, himself, or the Holy Spirit who would be present with his followers. It would always be just the one true God, Father, Son, and Holy Spirit, but this time in her manifestation as Spirit.

We know the one true God in these three manifestations. We don't know anything about the internal life of God, certainly not enough to make subdivisions of God's personality. We don't know anything about one "person" of God being "begotten," or "proceeding," from any other "person" or "persons." The doctrine of one God with three manifestations to humanity adequately expresses the union of God with humanity, first in the creation of humans and of the world, second in the person of Jesus, and third in the followers of Jesus. That's what the doctrine of the Trinity was intended to express by those who oversaw its early development.

Notes and Sources for Further Reading

James Joyce, *Ulysses* (Modern Library, 1961), p. 19.

For the discussion on the meaning of faith, and the difference between faith and belief, I am indebted to Roger Haight, S.J., and his book, *Dynamics of Theology* (Orbis Books, 1990, 2nd Ed. 2001), a marvelous work on what theology is and ought to be.

Friedrich Schleiermacher's principal work, published in 1820 and in a revised edition in 1830, is *The Christian Faith*. The English translation is *The Christian Faith* (T. & T. Clark, Edinburgh, 1928). It's a brilliant work, but not easy to find and rather hard to read. It repays the effort, however. Schleiermacher is thoughtful, subtle, and original, and he can follow an argument in a straight line better than anyone else I know.

William James's book, *The Varieties of Religious Experience* (Barnes & Noble Classics, 2004), is the text of the Gifford Lectures which James delivered at Edinburgh in 1901 and 1902. It's well-written, thoughtful, and fascinating to read. The quotation is from pp. 441-42.

John Henry Newman's *A Grammar of Assent* (Doubleday Image Books, 1955), written in 1870, is a very fine examination of how we know truth, particularly but not exclusively religious truth. Newman's approach is one of great common sense.

C. S. Lewis, *Mere Christianity* (Macmillan, 1943).

Francis S. Collins, *The Language of God* (Free Press, 2006).

Jack Miles wrote *God, a Biography* (Vintage Books, 1996), a serious and scholarly examination of the widely varying views of God found in the Hebrew Scriptures, at times wrathful, at times a leader in war, at times a family deity, and so forth. A very thoughtful book.

Hans Küng wrote an impressive study of the development of the idea of God in modern philosophy, *Does God Exist* (Crossroad Publishing, 1999).

A complete and thorough survey of the development of the doctrine of the nature of Jesus is found in Roger Haight's *Jesus, Symbol of God* (Orbis Books, 1999). Haight covers some of the same material, with less historical and scholarly detail, in *The Future of Christology* (Continuum, 2005), a book which develops a contemporary framework for thinking and reflecting on the nature of salvation through Jesus, the role of the Christian in that salvation, and the relationship of the Christian understanding of God's salvation to other religious traditions. Strongly recommended.

The quotation from James Alison is found in *Raising Abel* (Crossroad Publishing, 1996), p. 40 (emphasis added). This is a brilliant and powerful book by an author who views Jesus in the light of Girard's theories. Not to be missed.

X

LIVING BY THE FIVE COMMANDMENTS

"And behold, I am with you always, until the end of the age." (Mt 28:20)

As WE BEGIN THIS LAST CHAPTER, let me sum up the elements of my approach to Christianity through the five commandments of Jesus:

1. Life on earth is difficult for all of us human beings. We all begin life without culture or morals, and we must work to acquire and exercise self-control, basic skills, and specialized competencies by practice against resistance throughout life and through some suffering, and when we get good at these we get old and die.

2. Life on earth is made more difficult for all of us by the presence in our genes of the naturally selected anti-social behaviors of violence, kinship affinity, dominant-submissive behaviors, and acquisitiveness.

3. The social, cultural, and political institutions of the world, built upon the ancient human culture of sacrifice and its rituals and practices, have controlled and channeled these genetically based behaviors, not by opposing them, but by absorbing them into our institutions, laws, and customs.

4. Jesus of Nazareth, a young Jewish man of the early first century, was a teacher sent by God. Throughout his life he was guided and inspired by a full indwelling of God in his consciousness, which made him in a real sense divine. He taught us, among other things, that God is a loving father to all humans.

5. The central ethical teachings of Jesus, which are his five commandments, constitute a direct and specific instruction to men and women to resist and overcome our genetically based anti-social behaviors, and a specific description of the attitudes and actions which we are to put in their place.

6. In his teachings and in his life and death, Jesus attacked the world's culture of sacrifice and the genetically based behaviors which it had internalized, seeking to uproot them, to

reform humanity's public social, cultural, and political institutions, and to replace the culture of sacrifice with the kingdom of God.

7. The ethical demands of the five commandments of Jesus are difficult to follow, but, on reflection, we can see that we ought to accept and practice them for the good of the world and for our own good, and that they offer a way, perhaps the only way, to overcome humanity's most difficult problems.

8. It is by the overthrow of the culture of sacrifice and its replacement with the kingdom of God, which is the community of men and women who accept and practice the five commandments of Jesus, that Jesus redeems the world. That's what makes Jesus our redeemer and savior.

9. Jesus didn't accomplish his redemptive activity by himself alone. Rather, he began our redemption by gathering those who would follow his teachings, teaching them, inspiring them, and then entrusting them with continuing the task. Completing the redemption of humanity by putting the five commandments of Jesus into practice is the task of the followers of Jesus. Thus many men and women will participate in the redemption of the world.

Taken together, this is a somewhat unconventional view of Christianity, even though it is a view with strong support from the life and the teachings of Jesus himself. It isn't what most Christians have heard in church. It'll take some getting used to. But I believe an unconventional view of Christianity, such as the one presented here, may be more attractive to many of us than the conventional and traditional views.

Note that in this approach to Christianity, the Christian religion does its work in the world by natural human means, not by magic. With this approach, the problems of human life are those we see in ourselves and in the world around us, and those we learn from history, literature, evolutionary psychology, and cultural anthropology. These problems are not caused by a mythical Satan or by the sin of a mythical first man and woman. The remedy for these problems is the practice of the five commandments of Jesus. Their practice in personal life and their application to institutions of human society require the exercise of natural human intelligence, initiative, willpower, and courage. We can see a natural cause-and-effect relationship between our practice and application of the five commandments and the improvements in our own lives and in the lives of others which we seek. The practice of the five commandments builds character, freedom, and creativity in those who persist. There's no magic in this, only hard work.

There's a strangeness about this approach, and in all true Christianity, which must be identified, so that the elements of strangeness can be seen not to affect the plausibility or the credibility of the approach I have described. This strangeness arises because the life and teachings of Jesus contain at their center a jarring inversion of human values. A crucified criminal from an obscure province of the Roman Empire has become the central figure in a great world religion, divine in some way, and the redeemer of humanity. He called all who would follow him to be non-judging and humble, to refrain from violence and greed, and to forgive, and he then asserted that, with these difficult but apparently impotent virtues, his followers would fundamentally change the world. No wonder it seems strange. It was so from the beginning. As N. T. Wright observes, in one of his books about the apostle Paul,

> One of the central tensions in Paul's thought, giving it again and again its creative edge, is the clash between the fact that God always intended what has in fact happened and the fact that not even the most devout Israelite had dreamed that it would happen like this.

The mission of Jesus is strange. It's in many ways a surprise. But that doesn't affect its credibility or its attractiveness. Quantum mechanics is stranger still, but it's an accepted part of modern physics. As Chesterton once observed, a key is strangely shaped; but the fact that it's strange is irrelevant. What matters is that it fits the lock.

If this approach includes the least possible overt and public intervention by God in human affairs, as I believe it does, timing would be important. There would be a right time and place for the mission of Jesus. Jesus introduced his public ministry with the words, "The time is fulfilled, and the kingdom of God has come near; change your minds, and believe in the good news" (Mk 1:15). Paul put the same idea this way: "When the fullness of time had come, God sent his Son, born of a woman, born under the law, in order to redeem those who were under the law" (Gal 4:4-5).

Why was the early first century the "fullness of time"? Consider the following:

Before Jesus came, humanity had developed the basic moral rules of civilized society, of which the ten commandments of Moses are one example, and principles of justice, good faith, and magnanimity. The Israelites had developed a sophisticated monotheism. So Jesus didn't have to spend time teaching about these matters. Jesus was able to concentrate his teachings on his five commandments and on his new teachings about God, the elements of sacrificial culture, the kingdom of God, and his own central role. In the time of Jesus, the custom and practice of historical writing had developed and was widespread (consider not only the Gospels but also the histories of Thucydides, Josephus, and Livy), so the words and acts of Jesus could be recorded and transmitted with some accuracy and permanence, certainly not perfectly, but sufficiently for the task. It was helpful and perhaps essential for the survival and spread of the teachings of Jesus that for the two or three centuries immediately following his death, the Mediterranean world was relatively peaceful and prosperous, and travel and communication over long distances was possible and practical.

Consider that if all that was needed for the redemption of humanity was that the Son of God must become man and offer himself as an atoning sacrifice to God, that could've happened at any time. It could've taken place in 10,000 B.C. God would've then simply announced at some later time that it had taken place, as the Fall of Adam and Eve was announced to us long after it is said to have taken place. Only if the teachings of Jesus and their spread by natural human historical means were both critical elements of the redemptive activity of Jesus is there a "fullness of time," a time when the teachings could and would be heard, remembered, recorded, taught to others, and preserved and passed down from generation to generation.

Timing is also important for a renewed interest in and concentration on the five commandments of Jesus, and particularly on their application to public institutions. The time was not right for the latter until the modern era. For the first three centuries of Christianity, Christians generally had little or no influence in political and cultural matters within the Roman Empire. The question of applying the teachings of Jesus to public institutions rarely if ever arose. When the Roman Empire quite abruptly switched from the persecution of

Christians to the elevation of Christianity as the official religion of the Empire, under Constantine and his successors, Christians were in no position to resist, and the Christian church became in effect a part of the civil government. As a result, the Christian church could no longer oppose violence by the state, exclusion and persecution of those deemed enemies of the state, hierarchies and class distinctions of all kinds, or the concentration of wealth and power in the hands of the very few, and the church began its discreditable practice of using state power to enforce orthodoxy and persecute heretics.

From the fourth through the twelfth centuries, the Christian church was engaged in bringing kingdom after kingdom of pagans and barbarians into the church. It was thus necessary to concentrate on the ten commandments and on society's basic moral and cultural rules, to civilize the barbarians. During the same period, the Christian church was engaged in preserving the holy Scriptures and the writings of early Christians, as well as what it could of the writings of the Greek and Roman civilizations, and to do so had to teach its monks and clerics to read and write, then an otherwise rare ability. As men who could read and write were indispensable to the administration of civil government, clerics and monks generally came to staff all the centers of civil administration, such as they were. Church continued to be completely intertwined with state, and remained so until roughly the eighteenth century. From the early Middle Ages until the Protestant Reformation the Christian church was itself a highly centralized military power in Italy and a major political power in Europe.

Which brings us to the present day, more or less. I've been asked why, if the Christian church has been around for almost two thousand years, the application to our public institutions of the principal teachings of the Sermon on the Mount, the five commandments, hasn't been part of the Christian tradition. I suggest as an answer that there seem to be three prerequisites for a historical period in which the application of the five commandments of Jesus to social, cultural, and political institutions is a practical and realistic possibility: first, separation of church and state; second, responsive democracy with universal suffrage; and third, a general revulsion against violence. We are just now entering a historical period in which these three prerequisites are met.

Separation of church and state. Although the separation of church and state has its philosophical roots in the Middle Ages, it wasn't until after the destructive wars of religion which were fought in France, Germany, and England in the late sixteenth and early seventeenth centuries that separation from religion began to be seen as necessary for the survival of the modern nation-state. Separation of church and state became part of the United States Constitution in 1791 and is contained in the Universal Declaration of Human Rights adopted by the United Nations in 1948. Both protect the free exercise of religion, along with the rights of free speech, public assembly, and the free press, and both thus provide protection to those who on ethical grounds advocate changes in public policy. Both prohibit the establishment of any religion by the state. These rights permit Christians without civil power to speak truth to the civil power, and they prevent those who do so from using the power of the state to impose their religiously-based views upon others.

Responsive democracy with universal suffrage. Both England and the United States expanded voting rights from a small group of men with property, in the late eighteenth century, to more and more men in the nineteenth century, to women in the early twentieth century, and, in America, effectively to African-Americans only since the 1960s. Responsive democracy with universal suffrage provides a substantial responsible and potentially responsive audience, most of whom at any given time will not be holding political power, to whom the arguments of those seeking social, political, and institutional changes may be directed.

A general revulsion against violence. This, while less obvious, is an important prerequisite, because the intense emotions aroused by perceived threats to national security, justified or not, and the intense desire for retaliatory violence when an injury is received, overwhelm rational appeals for reform. We have seen a sea change on this front in the world in the last fifty years, and only much more recently and less firmly in the United States. War is now obsolescent or obsolete. In recorded history up until and including World War II, it was always possible for nation-states to expand and enrich themselves by military conquest. That's no longer the case.

As long as economic activity was principally agricultural, military forces could conquer land, and those working the land would stay on the land and accept the rule of the conquering power. Even as late as

1940, the economies of France and Poland were largely agricultural. But when people and their economic activities become separated from the land, as they have generally become in the last sixty years, successful expansion by military conquest has become extremely difficult, perhaps impossible. Partly as a result of this, the asymmetric warfare we've seen for the last sixty years favors an insurgent patriotic resistance over foreign occupying military forces of much greater power. Violence as conventional warfare no longer works. War is no longer a realistic instrument of policy. Europe has been without war (except in the Balkans) for over sixty years now, and the prospect of war between major European nations is now practically unthinkable. Since then, as I argued in Chapter 8, nonviolence has repeatedly shown itself superior to military force in changing the rule of nations.

These modern conditions indicate that the traditional Christian standard that Sermon on the Mount ethics can't be applied to the public institutions of the world was a historically-conditioned standard. It was arguably correct under the historical conditions prevailing throughout most of the history of the Christian churches. But those conditions have changed, and current conditions make application of the five commandments of Jesus to public institutions possible. To so apply them seems to me to be the appropriate continuation of the mission of Jesus in our times.

Returning to my approach to Christianity through the five commandments of Jesus, the question arises: How will you, the reader, respond to this approach? Some of you will want to think about it before making a commitment, because committing to it entails a decision to act on it. These readers will want to read other approaches, review the traditional doctrines, and discuss this approach with friends or in a study group. This is a thoughtful response. Some of you may wish to accept the five commandments and leave the theology to one side. I think it may be difficult to practice the five commandments as an ethical system without at the same time looking to Jesus as a model, an exemplar, a teacher, and a mediator of God's will, but it isn't impossible.

And some of you will be persuaded by this approach, and would like to read more about how you might go about pursuing the incorporation of the five commandments into your lives and into your religious activities. It's to this group of readers that the balance of this chapter is directed.

Let's talk first about adult conversion. It's a strong Christian tradition that one is born a Christian, and brought into a Christian church by infant baptism or by a childhood or adolescent acceptance of Jesus as Lord and savior. The Christian churches give basic instruction in Christianity in Sunday school or parochial school, and the basic instructions don't change much as we mature. They just seem to get less relevant to our lives and to the world as we see it, as we grow into adulthood. So we, or our children, drift away from the Christian churches.

At this point, as Juan Luis Segundo accurately observes, "There is only one mature way of facing up to this situation. At least once in our life we must try to make the hypothetical mental journey that precedes the decision to be a Christian." If you, a mature person, make this mental journey and decide to accept the teachings of Jesus and join in his redemptive activity, not on the authority of parents or teachers, but because of a personal judgment that Jesus is trustworthy and his teachings are good and true, you will have made an adult conversion.

The conversion to Jesus and his teachings is difficult. Let's not kid ourselves. The hard part of conversion to Jesus and his teachings isn't reaching the belief that there is a God, or concluding that the Gospels are reasonably authentic and accurate records of the life and teachings of Jesus, or even believing that Jesus rose from the dead. The hard part is committing ourselves to the required change of mind and deciding to take on the very difficult task of becoming nonviolent, non-judging, forgiving, humble, and detached from possessions.

The conversion to the change of mind and heart required by Jesus doesn't require a leap of faith. It requires courage, not a leap of courage, but steadfast courage. And none of us are sure enough in our hearts that we will have steadfast courage. That's why the person of Jesus, and the example of his life, is so important. That's why he didn't say "I have taught you the way, and the truth, and the life," but "I *am* the way, and the truth, and the life." We can reason our way to the correctness of a body of teachings, but we need a leader, and in this case the example of a real human leader who has already traveled the path, to make a commitment of steadfast courage.

Traditional Christianity has often urged conversion on people because, the traditional view holds, membership and participation in a Christian church is necessary for salvation, and getting into heaven should be each person's primary goal. This view may be suitable for children, but it isn't a mature view, and it isn't good theology. God wills that all men and women be saved, and God knows that many men and women have either never heard of Jesus or of the Christian churches, or have been repelled by the conduct of their representatives.

The reason for becoming a follower of Jesus shouldn't be simply the offer of personal salvation. Instead, it should be your desire to be an active participant in redeeming the world through the practice and application of the five commandments of Jesus. The advantage of being a Christian, a follower of Jesus, isn't that it gets you into heaven, as that is offered to all men and women, but that we Christians learn God's plan and can bring our abilities and talents to bear in our own ways on the implementation of God's plan. Christians are to be the light of the world, Jesus said. A light doesn't shine for itself only; rather, it illuminates all it shines upon. Christians are to be the yeast which leavens not itself but the whole loaf. To accept the call of Jesus in this way is to accept and undergo a new and mature conversion to Christianity. It is, among other things, making a commitment to be deeply other-directed and thus to grow in love and in the capacity to love.

What of the role of divine grace in our conversion to Christianity and in our lives as Christians? In Catholic parochial school, I learned at an early age that "grace" is a quantifiable though invisible and supernatural stuff, that we each have a "grace" account in heaven, and that the balance could be increased in specified increments by various pious practices and rituals. It was a transferable commodity, like currency, which could be applied at the will of the account-holder to the poor souls in Purgatory. Apparently the same teaching was common in Latin America; Juan Luis Segundo speaks of the "bank-deposit" form of common Catholic sacramental theology. This view is of course a wholly magical explanation of the use of sacraments and of pious practices. As Segundo says, by it the church "thoroughly negates its liberative commitment to the message of Christ."

There's a tendency in Christian teaching to describe grace as a thing which God gives to us, separate from the gifts of conversion and sanctification, so that we can by the power of grace receive the gifts of conversion and sanctification. In Protestant evangelical theology, the converting Christian must first receive grace from God before he or she can accept the revelation of Jesus as redeemer. Similarly, according to the Roman Catholic catechism,

> Faith is a gift of God, a supernatural virtue infused by him. *Before* this faith can be exercised, man must have the grace of God to move and assist him . . . . Believing is possible only by grace and the interior helps of the Holy Spirit.

Grace is thus described as a separate supernatural entity rather than as a simple relationship. I think this concept of grace is unnecessary and misleading.

The principal reason this confusing theology of grace was developed was to leave no question that the redemption of men and women by Jesus is the free gift of God, unearned and unmerited by us humans. After all, grace is simply another word for gift. But the theology of grace as a separate stuff isn't needed to protect this teaching. A simpler and more direct way to state the redemptive message is to say that Jesus *is* grace; he *is* the gift of God, for God opened his God-consciousness, and he was united with God in his life, his teaching, his death, and his resurrection. Jesus comes to each of us by the natural means of the spoken and written word. Thus is grace transmitted. Each of us responds to this gift, this grace, if, as and when we accept the person of Jesus as teacher and redeemer and commit to follow and practice his five commandments. Thus is grace received.

The act of believing and committing isn't based on an infused power separate both from the truths we believe and from the person to whom we commit. The truths which lead us to the decision of faith are a set of truths at which we have arrived by the natural processes of our reasoning intelligent minds and judgments. There is no "grace" separate from the message of Jesus itself. There is no "supernatural faith." We conclude, based on the evidence, that there was a person called Jesus; that he said what the Gospels record him as having said; that he lived the life the Gospels record him as having lived; and that he called each of us to restore our higher ideals, the virtues of his five commandments, to our working personal value structures. We concede, on the merits of his teachings, that this is a call to which it would be reasonable to respond affirmatively. This is all perfectly natural. Reason gets us this far, and no further. Now we must choose. If, after a gut-check, we choose to respond to the call of Jesus, to open our personal value structures to the higher values of the five commandments, and to commit to their practice, that's not simply an act of faith. It's an act of courage.

What of the spiritual life of Christians? What of growth in holiness? Does practicing the five commandments of Jesus in our personal lives and then working for their implementation in the institutions of the world have anything to do with the spiritual life? Actually, this activity *is* the Christian spiritual life. As Roger Haight expresses it,

> Action for social grace and justice in this world is of itself genuine spirituality that unites one to God. This is not an addition to or the consequence of Christian spirituality that is somehow defined as complete in other terms. Action in the world and history that resists social sin and is engaged in the construction of social grace out of love *is* Christian spirituality. Of itself, by the power of grace, it unites one to God.

Let's suppose that you have decided that you want to be a follower of Jesus, to study and to learn to practice the five commandments: How should you go about it? And what should be the result? The answer to these questions will change from time to time, as new problems, new opportunities, and new perspectives arise. I can only suggest how it should be done in the present day and set forth some observations and recommendations for how to go about it.

My first observation is that working directly for changes within the structures and practices of existing and established Christian churches is probably not the way to go at this time. Church institutions, like all long-lived institutions, and the professional clergy will generally be highly resistant to changes which would depart in any significant way from Christian church traditions and which are not supported in the professional training and formation of priests and ministers.

Generally, those seeking to learn, practice, and apply the five commandments of Jesus should do so within small groups of like-minded lay people, probably but not necessarily within an established Christian congregation. Small Christian groups should not be larger than can meet regularly in homes of the members or in the parish's library or meeting room, small enough that everyone can participate in the discussion and conversation, and close enough that shy people can be comfortable about speaking out, asking questions, and saying what's on their minds. Tens of thousands of such small Christian groups are active in the United States today. In most cases, you should be able to find an existing group and join it. With some effort and seeking out, new groups can be formed.

How do you, alone or in a small Christian group, begin formation as a Christian who desires to live by the five commandments? You should begin, obviously, with intensive study of the life and teachings of Jesus. The primary source is close reading and rereading of the Gospels. Not the Bible; most of the Bible is the Hebrew Scriptures. The Hebrew Scriptures are important for an understanding of the history and religious culture of the Christian churches, and for a grasp of the social and religious environment in which Jesus was born and raised, and worked and died. But they contribute little, except by negative contrast, toward an understanding of the five commandments of Jesus. Not the whole New Testament; most of the epistles say little about the life or the teachings of Jesus. While some of the epistles of Paul are beautiful, and many are profound, Paul's writing is often difficult and hard to interpret. And the less said about the book of Revelation the better.

Stick to the Gospels. Find a good commentary if you can. Unfortunately, I haven't been able to find any helpful exposition or commentary on the five commandments of Jesus (which is one reason why I decided to write this one). Expect to be baffled by some of the teachings of Jesus. I'm still looking for a good explanation of the parable of the unjust steward (Lk 16:1-9). With some other teachings, you may be tempted to ignore them or explain them away, as for instance the occasional references to weeping and gnashing of teeth. Stick with it. Jesus will often console and strengthen you – and sometimes surprise you.

While there are, as far as I know, no other books on the five commandments as such, there's a lot of good reading material on their particular virtues. If you wish to pursue this, you can expand your reading and discussion, either on your own or within a small group, to include good books on nonviolence, equality, humility, tolerance for other views and for other peoples, the problem of poverty in the world, and so forth. Such reading and discussion will deepen your understanding of the structural defects in our social, cultural, and political institutions and of the ways in which they have internalized the genetically based behaviors against which Jesus directed his five commandments.

Meanwhile, you should work at incorporating the five commandments into your own habitual ethical attitudes and practices. As in developing any habitual skill, changing your own mind to conform to the five commandments requires practice against the resistance of our instinctive habits and involves trial and error. The opportunity for practice arises every day. I pick up the newspaper and read about a local bank robbery. The perp is apprehended, and his picture, in jail clothing, is in the paper. I see that is once again a young black man. Unbidden negative thoughts about black people in general, and young black men in particular, automatically come to mind. If I'm trying to practice the five commandments, this is the time for practice. I try to bring to mind reasons for not judging this fellow. Probably he has no job; maybe he has a dysfunctional family situation; probably he is poorly educated; certainly he makes bad choices. Most of the other young black men in the area are employed and of good character; this fellow isn't representative of them, let alone of black people in general. So I can suspend judgment, which is what Jesus told us to learn how to do, and perhaps I can feel a little sorrow and pity for the fellow. Did I get it right? Who can tell? Did I eliminate prejudice from my habits? Certainly not. But every bit of practice like this gets me a little closer.

Similarly, when I see a movie or a TV show in which the hero is portrayed as struggling against villains of absolutely unredeemable evil, whom he finally defeats with violence, I recognize it as another telling of the myth of redemptive violence, and thus a simplistic falsehood. I reflect that there are no humans out there in the world who are unredeemable (for to think so is to put limitations of our own making on God's power and her love), and that violence, even in response to violence, isn't a solution to any situation. Bit by bit, inch by inch, we change our own minds. If we persevere in our choice to follow the five commandments of Jesus, we come ever closer to seeing things the way Jesus saw them. It sounds utopian, but it works. This is what Paul was talking about when he counseled us, "Let this mind be in you, which was also in Christ Jesus" (Phil 2:5).

I envision that many small Christian groups will evolve into continuing small Christian communities. For many such communities, its regular meetings would include not only study and discussion but common prayer. In some such communities, some meetings would include a Eucharistic service of consecration and distribution of bread and wine, the great symbol of the unity of Christians with Jesus and with each other. As I don't believe that Jesus intended priests to intermediate between God and man, or to officiate at a sacrifice, so I don't see any reason why any member of the group, man or woman, perhaps the host or hostess, couldn't say the words of remembrance of Jesus over the bread and wine and distribute communion to the others. This may be too radical for some members or some groups. Some groups may prefer to have an ordained priest or minister celebrate Eucharist with them, if one is available and willing, either as a member of the group or as an invited guest. Other groups may choose to elect one of their members as their liturgical leader, with the duty, and the authority given by the group, to consecrate and distribute the Eucharist in their community.

Where priests are in short supply, as they presently are in the Catholic Church, a willingness to consider Eucharistic consecration by the members themselves or by their chosen representative becomes more pressing. Progress in this direction is being considered even within the Catholic Church. In 2007, the Dutch Provincial Chapter of the Dominicans, an order of Catholic priests founded in 1207 and known formally as the Order of Preachers, published a paper, *Towards a Church With a Future,* setting forth the current situation in the Catholic Church in The Netherlands (not different, in terms of shortage of priests, from that prevailing in the American Catholic Church), and a careful review of the theology of church and of the Eucharist. The paper concluded that each Christian community should have and does have the right and power to select its own leaders to preside at real Eucharistic services within their community.

So the small Christian community I've described, if continuing and meeting regularly for discussions, study, action, and perhaps prayer and Eucharist, is really "church" for its members. What then of the traditional Christian parish or congregation? There are continuing practical problems of maintaining small Christian communities, such as stability over a long period, attraction and introduction of new members, professional support, and the provision of specialized services. The traditional Christian congregation or parish is usually perfectly suited to supply these needs.

A congregation or parish is a stable and enduring institution in a way in which a small Christian community can't be. It can offer specialized services, such as the education of children and the continuing education of adults, which the smaller group can't offer. It can provide a larger community and a larger venue for public celebration of baptisms, marriages, and funerals. It has a professional staff which can provide professional counseling and special ministry to the troubled, the sick, and the bereaved, and guidance in the formation and continuation of the small Christian groups themselves. It generally employs a professional pastor or rector who preaches weekly to his or her congregation. So I suggest that it will be helpful for a small Christian community to be closely associated with a traditional Christian congregation, particularly if the pastor or rector and the professional staff of the congregation approve of small communities, regard them as real Christian churches, and accept the role of the congregation in providing long-term continuity and special services support to the small communities.

Is there a preferred denomination to choose for your Christian parish or congregation? I would suggest a traditional Protestant or Catholic parish that provides the principal traditional signs of Christian service: Baptism, Eucharist, and the ministry of the word. A small Christian group may be less comfortable in a congregation which is aggressively fundamentalist or evangelical, or too vigorously fighting the battles of the past against evolution or against gays and lesbians. But the parishes of the traditional denominations are all Christian, and the choice is more a matter of personal preference than of doctrine. You should look for a congregation with a welcoming, active, and spirited group of parishioners and one which encourages freedom and exploration on the part of its people. Such a congregation may well be the home of the small Christian community you seek, or you may find that you with others can form one within the parish, so the attitude of the clergy of the parish toward such innovations may be an important factor.

Let's turn finally to the action-oriented activities of individuals and small Christian communities in working for the application of the five commandments of Jesus to public social, cultural, and political institutions. There are a myriad of possible applications; we saw only a few of them in Chapter 8. Individuals and small Christian communities will discover the issues which they wish to study and pursue, and the means they wish to employ. Some may work for the alleviation of poverty. Some may work for inter-racial justice, or inter-ethnic understanding. Some may work for the reform of the criminal justice system and its prisons. Some may teach in Christian schools or Sunday schools. There are many things to do.

As we, alone or in small Christian groups, deepen our understanding of the teachings of Jesus, particularly his five commandments, with continuing study, discussion, prayer, and action, we will begin to understand more clearly the defects and injustices in our social, cultural, and political institutions. As we share these insights and perspectives with each other, reinforce and deepen our collected insights, and go public with our arguments and our conclusions, there will eventually come into being a shift in the general view of the affected local or national population. When that occurs, defective patterns and practices in our public institutions can be corrected in light of the new views held by the relevant population. This is an important way of applying the five commandments to our public institutions.

As we saw in Chapter 3, it's the incorporation of the anti-social genetically based behaviors of humans into the great public institutions of society, particularly the nation-state, which makes these institutions the great oppressors of human freedom and creativity. The five commandments of Jesus are directed precisely against these behaviors. The application of the five commandments to the correction of social, cultural, and political institutions, and the eradication of these behaviors from them, under pressure from people who have internalized the five commandments in their personal lives, will change these institutions. This will release the freedom and creativity of the men and women living within these institutions. It will redeem the institutions and the people living within them. And this is the true coming of the kingdom of God.

Notes and Sources for Further Reading

The quotation from N. T. Wright is from his excellent short book, *Paul in Fresh Perspective* (Fortress Press, 2005), p. 54.

An important late medieval argument for separation of church and state is found in a book by Marsilius of Padua, *Defensor Pacis* (University of Toronto Press, 1986). The argument of the earliest American advocate of separation is set forth in Edwin S. Gaustad's *Liberty of Conscience: Roger Williams in America* (Judson Press, 1991).

Segundo's observation on conversion is found in *Grace and the Human Condition* (Orbis Books, 1973), p. 3. His discussion of the "bank-deposit" explanation of grace is found in *The Sacraments Today* (Orbis Books, 1974), pp. 92-93, 101-104. The quotation is from p. 93.

The quotation from the *Catechism of the Catholic Church* (Doubleday Image Books, 1995) is from Sections 153-54.

The quotation from Roger Haight is found in Francis S. Fiorenza and John P. Galvin, eds., *Systematic Theology: Roman Catholic Perspectives, II* (Fortress Press, 1991), p. 139.

The paper of the Dutch Dominicans, *Towards a Church With a Future,* or *Church and Ministry*, is available under the Special Documents section at NCRonline.org.